MY FATHER'S DREAM

MY FATHER'S DREAM

Life in Palestine under the British Mandate

by
Harriett Goodman

with

Evelyn Julia Kent

Published in 2001
by
Evelyn Kent Associates
7 Savernake Court, Stanmore, England. HA7 2RA

Copyright © Harriett Goodman & Evelyn Julia Kent

Printed and bound in Great Britain by
Antony Rowe Ltd, Chippenham, Wiltshire

ISBN 0 9523716 85

A CIP Catalogue record for this book
is available from the British Library

Authors' note: This is a true story. As it has been told from memory
some of the names and incidental details may not be accurate.

*Dedicated to my most severe critics
and my best friends,
my dearly loved children
and grandchildren.*

'As my father planted for me,
so I plant for my children.'

Contents

———✦———

Insert of photographs and newspaper cuttings of the time

Front cover painting by Migs Goodman

Please note: In the transliteration of Hebrew into English, any word which includes *ch* uses the Scottish pronunciation of *ch* as in Lo*ch*.

Acknowledgements

I owe a great debt of gratitude to everyone who has given their time and expertise so generously.

The late Michael Davies assisted with erudite analysis of letters and events. His scholarly work will be sadly missed.

The late Rabbi Michael Leigh, who was my teacher and mentor, advised on religious background.

Advice on flight and travel background was given by Sylvia Goodman, Graham Chamberlain and Terry Charman.

Eli Baron, David and Gina Schwarzmann helped me to understand and transliterate Hebrew words.

Sympathetic editing was ably given by Greg Riener and John O'Toole. Hazel Davies and Daphne Young read the proofs and offered invaluable advice.

Computer experts David Morgan and especially Paul Baron set up the final text for the book. Danny Gold and Erica Osmond worked meticulously on the last proof reading.

Frank Entwistle, as ever, gave me correct spellings, support and wise counsel.

Throughout, Maurice Kanareck was there to assist with research, to verify facts and offer his invaluable know-how.

I relied as always on Sally Woolf, my daughter, who is my all time help.

Finally, my thanks and love to Harriett Goodman whose original letters and reminiscences have been the backbone to her story. *Evelyn Julia Kent*

Preface

Somehow I must convey that each part of my life was special. My life in New Haven was made up of being a member of a large close-knit family, not only of my parents and siblings, but many aunts, uncles, first cousins and both sets of grandparents, but also many extended members such as great aunts and uncles, second and third cousins.

When many years later I returned to New Haven with my children they asked, 'Mummy, is everyone in New Haven your cousin?' Wherever we went people asked, 'Are you Harriett's children? Well, I'm your cousin!' So apart from the normal childhood pleasures, there was the joy of being a younger child in an enormous, warm, friendly, extended family (all over Connecticut, Massachusetts, Rhode Island, New Jersey and New York).

Then came my later teens in Palestine. I have always maintained that there cannot be many young people who had such a fascinating, joyous time maturing into a woman. The social, emotional, intellectual stimulation of living in a country where everyone has a vision and works for it is a special way of life.

Built on the great security I carried from my American and strong family conditioning, I was open to enjoying the learning and pleasures of a new environment. The fascination of people from various countries with multi-cultural backgrounds and a variety of mother tongues extended my general understanding of the world.

Having reached the venerable age of eighty-three, I have succumbed to the request of my family and friends to finally get this story written. Without their encouragement, and the interest and help of Evelyn Kent, this book would not have seen the light of day. As I am reliant on my memory, my recall may be different from that of others who remember the events and people of whom I write.

Harriett Goodman

MY FATHER'S DREAM

PROLOGUE
(1874 – 1919)

So long ago. Part of my history is not mine at all but of my father and his father. Are the dreams of the fathers visited on the children? Is it that they wish for a secure future for their offspring when it was denied to them, or that they live out their dreams through their children? All the same, as youngsters we are unaware of the energies that spur our parents to protect and nurture us as they place us on pathways that mould us for our future.

I am inordinately proud of my parentage. My father, Jacob Lyon Gold, was a man of vision. He was born 1874 in Radeshkevitz, Russia, where anti-Semitism was prevalent and pogroms well established occurrences. He grew up in an atmosphere of religious discrimination while the Socialist revolution was gradually gathering momentum. Like all Russian Jews, Jacob Lyon yearned for a better, certainly safer, existence.

He was stalwart in his Judaism. When conscripted into the Russian army he never ate meat. If other soldiers de-bagged him for a laugh, he laughed alongside. Daily he recited morning prayers from the pocket Hebrew prayer book that he always carried. Whilst he served his time in the army he was good-humoured and unwavering in his faith. He came out the same Jew he went in.

By the time my father was a young man of twenty-three Theodore Herzl had convened the First Zionist Congress in

13

Basle in 1897. Reports of this and subsequent Zionist Congresses must have lifted his spirits with the idea of Zionism, which started to take shape amongst his contemporaries. A Jewish homeland safe from persecution was the dream of all Zionists. Russian Jews began to pioneer settlements in Palestine, turning themselves with difficulty from lawyers and doctors into farmers.

In Russia restrictions against Jews in education, law and medicine, increased their yearning for freedom from Russian tyranny. The new century only brought more terrible pogroms. Eventually my forebears made plans to emigrate. Like countless others, the Gold family began to gather what little resources they possessed in order to leave Russia.

The first of my family to make the hazardous journey to the land of the free was Great Grandfather Gross with his family, followed some years later by my Grandfather Gold with his wife, five younger sons and two daughters. They arrived in America during the first decade of the twentieth century.

By this time their eldest son, my father, was manager of a large Russian estate and had married Sarah Freda Meltzer, ten years his junior. They had three little girls, Rhea, Leah and Rose. Because of these family ties, my father did not have the finances to follow his family immediately. Possibly my mother, Sarah, did not wish to leave her parents now that she had children of her own. Perhaps Jacob Lyon, a true Zionist drawn to the idea of settling in the Holy Land, was biding his time for the right opportunity to go to Palestine. Whatever the reason, they remained behind in Belorussia.

Impending war in Europe and turmoil in Russia finally compelled my father to leave Minsk without his young wife and children. Despite his vision of Jewish people in their own homeland he turned, not towards Palestine where there was general unrest, but to the United States. Encouraged by letters from the family vanguard he joined thousands of immigrants on their way to Ellis Island.

He arrived in 1912 speaking Russian, Yiddish and Hebrew but little English. Nevertheless, he had spirit, energy and commitment to succeed. He joined the workforce in a pickling factory. One day, frustrated at trying to make himself understood, a rare anger built up as he exploded in Russian, 'How dare you laugh at me! *You* don't understand a word I'm saying!' His anger gained him respect from his contemporaries but it also gave impetus to his English. Soon he had enough command of the language to become the foreman.

He was now in a position to provide for his young family to join him. My mother and older sisters made the arduous journey to be reunited with my father and his family in 1913.

On 14th June 1914 there was rejoicing when Sarah gave birth to Sol. At last a son.

Jacob Lyon Gold (whom by now everyone called J.L.) settled his family seventy-eight miles north of New York in New Haven, Connecticut, where my parents' wholesale dairy business prospered. They were able to set up a secure home into which I was born on 11th June, 1917. My baby sister, Esther, was born there on 27th April, 1919.

It was a home where my father nurtured his dream for many years and finally brought it to fruition.

CHAPTER 1

New Haven (1917 – 1924)

I was born in New Haven, Connecticut. And why not? My father said that was where all the best people came from. My home town, on the east coast of America and north of New York, had grown from an early settlement started by the founding fathers into a thriving industrial city. Around the central green stood three wooden churches, while the white stone town hall, library and campus of Yale University were part of my background scenery. I was a real American kid, free as the day and full of hope. Brightness seemed to seep through the walls of our home.

My father, whom everyone called J.L., was intelligent and alive to new ideas. He was also an astute business man, making a good living with his own wholesale dairy. He was known as the 'butter and egg' man.

We lived in tree-lined Dwight Street, a typical avenue of American houses with lawns to the pavement. Our red-brick house consisted of two storeys, a basement and an attic, with a porch running along the front. This was where we children fooled around on the hammock that father reserved for himself every Saturday afternoon for a snooze.

The house held enough bedrooms to accommodate a growing family. My older sisters Rhea, Leah and Rose were born in Russia. When my elder brother, Sol, was born in America the family sighed with relief that they had a son and heir. Consequently, when I was born on 11th June 1917 as the fourth girl no one minded. Baby Esther arrived twenty-two months later to complete the Gold family.

My eldest sister, Rhea, was an attractive brunette. She possessed a bedroom of her own. When I was little, she would sneak cookies to tempt me to run errands for her. Her sweet tooth meant she was the only one of us inclined to be plump.

'Papa's told me he doesn't like fat girls,' she confided when she was in her late teens. 'If I lose weight he has promised to buy me a leopard skin coat.'

These were all the rage at the time and she was quite determined to have one. It took her months of self-denial to gain J.L's approbation, but finally we were all admiring her new coat.

Leah had to share a bedroom with her younger sister, Rose. Leah was petite, absolutely stunning and the most strong-willed of us all. She had everything and she knew it! Good looks, brains and spirit. With her blue-black hair, olive skin and dark eyes we thought she looked like the Queen of Sheba when she put her hair up. On the other hand, Rose was fair, pretty and very sweet-natured, which she had to be, sharing with Leah.

I was a real skinny tomboy, just happy to be part of the Gold family. But I always felt put out when one of my uncles continually teased me, comparing me to my little sister, Esther, the dark-eyed, black haired beautiful child.

'Esther is so pretty,' he said. 'A real Gold. But where do you come from?'

'I'm from New Haven,' I said indignantly. 'I am Harriett Ida Gold.'

He rubbed his chin thoughtfully.

'Ah, you do look like your older sister, Rose, with such fair colouring and blue eyes. I suppose you must be a Meltzer, like your mother's family.'

That seemed to settle the matter.

Leah was very fashion conscious and often tried on Rose's clothes. She even wore them. One morning the whole household was disturbed by screams and shouts emanating from their bedroom.

'That's mine! I want to wear that today!' shouted Rose, finally out of patience with her demanding elder sister.

'Get up earlier then!' shrieked Leah. 'It's on me now.'

We could hear them tussling around the room, trying to drag the clothes off each other. It was a real ding-dong. In exasperation, J.L. tore up the stairs and burst into their room.

'Right,' he said, flinging open the wardrobe. 'Whose is this?'

'It's mine,' said Leah sheepishly. He flung the dress at her.

He was in such a rage that both girls stood aghast as he grabbed clothes from the wardrobe and threw them out, dividing them on to each bed. He rounded on them.

'As from today, you never share. If you want to borrow something you ask the day before. Is that clear?'

We had never seen him so angry. We girls knew this was the bottom line. After that day my younger sister, Esther, and I never argued. We just agreed to disagree.

I adored my good-natured brother, Sol, and wanted to be with him all the time. If he went out to friends, I would trail after him into the street until he got fed up with me and urged me to 'Go home!' Then Mama would come out on to the porch and shout, 'Take her with you.' He would sigh, take my hand and allow me to go along with him.

Our house was equipped with all modern conveniences. A large Frigidaire stood in the kitchen, filled with food and supplying ice for the hot summers. In winter, the central heating came from a self-feeding furnace which sent warm air permeating around the house through hot air grills. When a delivery of fuel arrived, one of us had to stand outside and count the sacks of coal shunted into the coal-hole on the sidewalk. Sometimes the coal man accidentally emptied out a sack of unwashed coal which the furnace decided to devour the very minute we were expecting visitors. Sticky, black dust spewed out through the open grills causing everyone to have hysterics. Mama despaired as soot settled over tablecloths, plates, ornaments and furniture alike.

'Do something!' she shouted as we raced to the kitchen. 'Rhea, Leah, fetch the dusters. Rose, use the dustpan and brush. Harriett, get the feather duster. Come on Esther, you can help too.'

'Why can't Sol help?' I whined as I tried to clean up the window ledge, smearing my face with smuts.

'I've got five daughters. Your brother has better things to do!' Mama retorted.

We girls set to, madly trying to clear away the debris of smuts flying out of the wall grills. The whole house filled with coal dust. Everything had to be swept and cleaned.

'The nets will have to be washed tomorrow,' said Mama helplessly wiping her forehead as we heard the visitors approaching our front door.

Next day, all nets were taken down to be washed and dried on curtain stretchers in the attic. On washdays the attic was the drying room for linen and bedding. Our underwear was always hung outside to dry, even during icy winter-time when stiffly frozen long-johns, union suits and petticoats stretched like cardboard cut-outs right across our back yard.

On Sundays, J.L's parents, brothers, sisters and their families made the journey from Massachusetts, Rhode Island and parts of Connecticut to visit us. Cousins of various ages came along too, so we grew up knowing each other well. I was very proud of my relatives and revelled in the fun of the weekly reunions. Like many large Jewish families with a strong feeling of kinship, they would sit around the table, laughing, joking, exchanging news, happy to be together safely in the land of the free.

My mother, Sarah Freda, was a wonderful housekeeper, the epicentre of our household. She cheerfully catered for the crowd who filled her home over weekends. She must have felt sad sometimes since her own family, the Meltzers, were still enduring difficult times in Russia, but she said little about it. She was devoted to J.L.

On the eve of Sabbath, when the first star appeared in the sky, we waited quietly while Mama lit the candles, covering her eyes in silent prayer. Then Papa made 'Hamotzi', which is a thank you prayer over bread and wine; a Friday night ritual in every observant Jewish family. Afterwards he would read aloud from his prayer book the Hebrew psalm *'A woman of worth, who can find?'* eulogising his wife as *'a virtuous woman beyond the price of rubies'.* Mama would chuckle and give him a kiss. We knew they loved each other deeply and were sure of their faith. We were less certain.

'What kind of Jew should you be?' we asked father one morning.

He sat back in his chair and surveyed us with his smiling eyes.

'When I lived in Russia, we didn't eat cornflakes for breakfast. We didn't have telephones, or even electricity. It was easy to be a Jew. So what I'm asking you children is, if you can be an eighty per cent Jew, why be a thirty-five per cent one?'

We shifted around in our chairs not exactly understanding.

'Look, no one forces you to eat ham or bacon,' he went on. 'No one forces you to carry money or take a trolley-car on the Sabbath. But if the telephone rings then - '

'We pick it up?' I interrupted.

He nodded and that seemed the whole explanation.

It was the custom of my parents to hold open house every Friday night for friends. Often young scholarship men from Yale, impecunious Jewish students, came to visit. They liked to be with a Jewish family on Friday nights and enjoy a good meal. These young men were intellectuals, generally studying Law or Medicine. Many, like my father, held fervent ideas on Zionism and dreamt of a Jewish homeland. When we were little we peeped at them through the banisters, hearing the sometimes heated discussions going on long into the night. Often prominent Zionists visited our house to have deep discussions with J.L.

'We Jews are the people of the Torah, the bible. The land the Almighty gave us is where we should make our home,' said one.

'Why? We have made a good life here. To be Jewish we can live anywhere - we don't have to go to Palestine. In any case, most of it is either barren desert or swamp-infested, unfit for cultivation let alone the life-style we enjoy in America,' argued another.

'So who said life should be easy? We work at it. We build drains and water-courses. We make the desert bloom! We know we can do it. Our Kibbutz Deganya is already a flourishing settlement.'

'Even swamp land belongs to somebody. The Jewish National Fund (JNF) is raising money to buy land from the locals. There are plenty of land owners happy to sell such unproductive plots,' reasoned another.

Every weekend after that we children were co-opted to collect nickels and dimes in the blue and white JNF boxes, which we shook vigorously on our neighbours' porches. Papa, in his turn, bought small plots of land in the undeveloped area of Herzlia and gave certificates of ownership to Barmitzvah boys, who thought the present of a piece of paper was crazy and often threw it away.

'Thank you, Uncle,' said Joe, my favourite cousin, who had just received such a certificate on his thirteenth birthday. 'What is it for?'

'Your future,' said my father seriously. 'Small plots grow into valuable pieces of real estate. Hold on to it, it will be worth a lot some day.'

Gradually, the Jewish population of New Haven changed its direction, moving up-town as the hard-working immigrants became more affluent. One of the local churches was now converted into a synagogue for the enlarged congregation. On Saturday mornings, Papa walked there taking any of his children who wanted to go along with him. I went through religious patches. Sometimes I liked to be at the synagogue service where I could watch my father, wrapped in his prayer shawl, absorbed in prayer. Other times I decided I had other things to do. Anyway, the minutiae of religious observance was not all that important to us children, we could take it or leave it. We knew we were Jewish.

CHAPTER 2

Zunder School (1924 – 1927)

The wholesale business that Father owned was called 'Gold's Dairy'. Eventually he set up his own retail outlet called *'The Model Creamery'*, just filled to overflowing with delicious milk products; cream cheeses, salted herrings, smoked salmon and olives, enough to make one's mouth water. Later he opened another shop *'The Supreme Delicatessen'* which specialised in meat products such as salami, chopped liver sausages with pickled cucumbers. We had great fun in his shops because we were allowed to help ourselves to anything we liked. Occasionally we were even permitted to help serve behind the counter.

'Gold's Dairy' owned a huge shire horse called Nellie. She was a gentle, docile animal who pulled the wagon used for daily deliveries. We all adored her. She was stabled just along the road from the dairy and was father's pride and joy. He would groom her lovingly, occasionally letting me help comb her tail. Then he would lift me on to her broad, brown back, my little legs straddling either side as I clung on to her thick mane while she ambled around her paddock.

Somehow my mother found time to help run the business from the dairy office. Our school, Zunder School, was around the corner from Gold's Dairy, so at noon-time every school day we returned to the warehouse for something to eat before afternoon lessons. I always saved some little treat for Nellie, who gently nudged me as she accepted offerings of apples or carrots.

One lunchtime we raced back from school to find my father and mother standing in the yard admiring an automobile, a black van with a flat roof and the letters GOLD`S DAIRY written in white and gold on the side.

'What do you think of progress?' asked J.L. proudly.

I was horrified. Progress was one thing, Nellie was another. I burst into tears, terrified of what was going to happen to her. Papa took my hand and led me over to the stable where Nellie stood contentedly munching hay. He patted her neck affectionately.

'Nellie is an old lady, but she will stay with us for the rest of her days,' he said. 'She will enjoy a long, well-earned retirement. Just like I am going to have.'

The van had to be started with a handle to crank up the engine. On fine days it quickly spun into life. Other times, especially in cold weather, the engine spluttered, moaned and then died.

'Nellie never let me down like this!' yelled my father in one of his rare rages.

*

In all weathers, I skipped alongside Sol to school. When he was out of sight of our house, he would yank his belt from his trousers (which managed to stay up just the same) tie the belt around his pile of books and swing them over his shoulder, just to be one of the boys.

With my Buster Brown haircut and bobby socks, I was like all the other girls in Miss Lampson's class, Third Grade. Miss Lampson was the sweetest roly-poly lady imaginable. All her lessons were fun and since reading and writing came easily to me I enjoyed being at school. At the end of the year I progressed to Miss Clarke's Fourth Grade class feeling very pleased with myself.

Miss Clarke was a tall, kindly teacher who did not frighten me at all. I was so good at English that spelling tests soon lost their importance and I neglected even to look at the weekly lists we had to learn. Eventually, of course, I failed to get full marks two weeks in a row and was quite unprepared for Miss Clarke's anger.

'Why aren't you learning your spellings, Miss?' she accosted me.

I chewed gum nonchalantly and shrugged.

'That's it, Harriett! Do not think I will have such a slacker in my class. Go at once to the principal, Miss Allen. She can deal with you. And take that gum out of your mouth!'

My mouth hung open in surprise, but I was tight-lipped when I knocked tentatively on Miss Allen's door. She was a good-looking, imposing woman, dressed in a long black dress with pristine white collar and cuffs. My mother had taken to her like a kindred soul and was entirely satisfied to entrust the education of all her children to Miss Allen's tutelage. The headmistress adjusted her pince-nez to look at me severely, studying me silently for some minutes.

'What do you think your mother would feel about your laziness?' she eventually enquired.

I did not reply. I had the feeling that she and my mother had been discussing my attitude to school work without my knowing.

To my stunned consternation she continued, 'Harriett Gold, you are to be demoted to Miss Lampson's class. You will sit in the last row and complete spelling tests every day. After each correct test of fifty words, you may then move up a seat until you reach the top of the class. Only then will you have earned the privilege of being in Fourth Grade.'

Scared out of my wits, I ran out of school not wanting to see or talk to anyone. Where could I hide? The dairy seemed a good place so I scooted up to the second floor where the family provisions and vegetables were stored and hid in a half empty apple barrel.

'They'll think I'm lost - or dead,' I thought. 'Then everyone will be sorry!'

But the foreman had spied me sneaking away and I was soon yanked out of the barrel, taken to my parents and given a good hiding for upsetting everybody.

In Miss Lampson's class each day I had to do spelling tests. I was only allowed to move up a seat when every spelling was correct. Thirty six seats. I had never been inclined to concentrate, but boy did I work avidly! It took two weeks to get back into my class, but it was a lesson well taught. And I never chewed gum in school again.

*

When winter came with snow covering the rooftops and sidewalks, we trudged to school in our Arctics pulled on over our shoes, mufflers wrapped around our necks, heads snug in knitted pom-pom hats. Bitterly cold air chilled our breath to look like smoke. At school, preparations were going ahead for the end of term celebrations. I sang carols alongside my classmates and helped make decorations for the Christmas tree. I asked Mama if we could have a tree in our house, but she refused.

'At this time of year we have Chanukah. That is our festival,' she explained. 'We celebrate the eight days of Chanukah to commemorate that the oil lamp, which held only enough oil to burn for one night, burned steadily for eight full nights in the restored Temple in olden times.'

When the festival arrived we children took turns each evening to light the coloured candles in the Chanukiah. One, plus the shamash, for the first night, up to a full eight for the

27

last night as the miracle grew. They were small, delicate candles that to our disappointment soon burned down and went out.

'These tiny lights last for only half an hour, just to remind us of the little light of freedom that glows inside all of us.' said Papa.

After dinner we each received gifts or *Chanukah gelt,* money we could save to buy whatever we liked. We sang songs and retold the story of Judas Maccabaeus. How in ancient times he had recaptured Jerusalem from the Syrians and re-dedicated the Temple to the Almighty.

'It is the story of right over might,' said Papa. 'In those days we fought to regain our own land. We are going to build a country for ourselves once more. You must remember, we are a people like all other people. We are farmers, taxi-drivers and dustmen. We are doctors and teachers. And, when necessary, we are also fighters. Jews can reside anywhere they like in the world, but they must have a country of their own. One day *we* will live in it.'

*

As the seasons changed, so did our lifestyle.

'There's a lot to be said for the summer house,' said Mama, as we rolled up the carpets, covered all the furniture with dust sheets, locked the windows, pulled the blinds down and closed our house in Dwight Street for the vacation.

We spent the summer at our beach house in Woodmont, Milford, Connecticut. It stood on the top of a hill overlooking Long Island Sound. The two storey wooden cottage could sleep twenty, if you counted the visitors bedding down on the floors. It was not winterised, so we opened it in June and lived there until the beginning of September. At night, when it became hot and humid, we children slept out on the porch, staring at the stars. By day, we swam in the Sound and played games on the pebbly beach.

We did not have to travel far for provisions. There was a small grocer's shop nearby. Melnick, the baker, arrived at the house daily with fresh pumpernickel bread and hot bagels. Local farmers delivered fresh produce.

With no school for the long holidays, we revelled in a sense of freedom and fun that my parents must have mused upon, remembering their Russian past.

CHAPTER 3

The Barmitzvah (1928 – 1931)

My older sisters, Leah, Rhea and Rose, were growing into attractive young women. As always, they vied with each other to look fashionable.

'What will Papa think?' asked Rhea one Saturday morning as she, Leah and Rose admired themselves upstairs in a long mirror.

They were wearing up to the minute dresses with dropped waists and short skirts that showed off their slim, shapely legs. The minute they heard father returning from synagogue they went nervously downstairs to greet him. He stopped in his tracks as he turned to see them standing on the stairs, one above the other.

'Don't you three look gorgeous!' he exclaimed, as they came down and threw their arms around him.

In the afternoon, when we were all lounging on the porch in the shade, Papa looked up from the hammock where he always napped.

'What are you girls looking for in a husband?' he asked, making us all giggle.

'What did you look for in a wife, Papa?' I asked.

We urged him on. He looked thoughtful, took his time, then waggled his finger at us.

'I looked for three things. A pretty face, so I wouldn`t have to look elsewhere.' He grinned at us. 'And I would have pretty children.'

We screamed with delight.

'That's only one,' said Rhea.

'Nice in-laws, so my wife would be well-bred and know how to bring up my children properly.'

We felt indignant.

'We are brought up properly!' exclaimed Leah.

Papa concurred, then said, 'And - money. But there's a problem with this.'

We could not see much of a problem. We felt these were good aims and that Papa had found everything he had looked for. We waited impatiently for him to continue.

'The problem is you can't have everything you want. And so - I dropped the money.' He spread his arms expansively. 'I can make that myself!'

'Why did you drop the money?' Rose wanted to know.

Papa chuckled. 'Your mother came with a dowry but, for some reason when we signed the wedding contract, it did not materialise. I'm still waiting!' He roared with laughter, then became more serious. 'You have to give up something. You decide. No-one gets everything they want in life.'

Mama, the quiet, wise one, came out to see why we were all so amused, but he pulled her to him and said no more.

'I know what you are saying J.L.' Mother tweaked his moustache. 'You didn't do too badly!'

*

Since my younger sister, Esther, and I were less than two years apart we always slept together in the small bedroom, bouncing about on cherry-wood beds, holding on to the tall posts at the end, before falling asleep. We shared the table in-between that held books and treasures. There was a matching tallboy with a swinging mirror and a chest of drawers for our clothes. In our early days we were even dressed alike. Twice a year Mother took us on an outing to Shartenburg's store in New Haven. For winter we were equipped with matching

31

sweaters and skirts, socks and shoes, mine always two sizes larger. In springtime we were each bought six identical pretty print dresses with matching bloomers. There was no school uniform so we wore our dresses to school as well. But as I became more grown up, I objected.

'Do I have to wear the same as Esther?' I complained.

'Sure you do. It makes you look very cute,' Mama assured me.

I must have looked downcast, so she added, 'When you move up to Junior High things will be different.'

Esther had followed me into Zunder School, two grades below. She began to follow me everywhere. When she was a baby I had trailed after Sol until, in desperation, he had allowed me along with him and the boys. Now it was her turn to run after me.

'Go home!' I shouted, running out to join the other kids to play Hopscotch, Double Rope or One, Two, Three O'Leary. But she stuck behind me until mother saw and shouted 'Take her with you!' So then I had to drag her around with me. I sighed to myself. Esther always got what she wanted. Everyone thought she was adorable. When she was small she captivated the world.

When she attempted to pronounce words in her babyish voice everybody cooed over her. But if I tried to talk like that Mama became angry with me.

'Speak properly!' she chastised.

Occasionally I still managed to persuade Sol to take me with him, especially when I found out his gang were exploring a house being built nearby.

'Chase me!' I cried, as I ran into the empty building.

I heard the boys clattering after me as I tried to escape them. Suddenly the floor gave way under me. My body twisted, my legs sprawled behind me and I fell head first through an open trap door in to the cellar. I lay moaning on the concrete floor, confused and concussed.

'Harriett, where are you?' I heard Sol shouting but I could not speak.

'She's down here,' said one of the boys, peering over the edge.

'Come on, get up!' ordered Sol.

'I can't see any steps.' I managed to sit myself up and look around.

'Hold on to me then,' Sol instructed as he lowered himself through the hole, hands hanging down with the boys sitting on his legs.

I was able to pull myself up to reach his hands which clasped mine firmly. Then with a lot of shouted commands: 'Hang on!' 'Pull her up slowly!' 'Got her, careful now!' 'Harriett, you dope!' they managed to drag me back up.

My face was sore and bruised, but I was determined not to cry.

'Don't you dare say anything when we get home,' Sol warned.

At the start of every food season, my father would bring home a whole box of the latest item, such as grapes or strawberries. We children were allowed to eat as much as we liked. His purpose was simple. If we had our fill, we would not beg our mother incessantly for this particular food. On the evening of my accident as a special treat he produced an enormous halvah, a delicious honey and almond desert. Only I refused to eat it. My face hurt too much but I did not dare to say anything.

'Whatever is the matter with you? Have you got a toothache?' Leah demanded. It was apparent she would like to be a dentist. I shook my head.

'She just wants attention,' said Rhea. 'Leave her be.'

But Rose sensed it was something more. Eventually she persuaded Sol to tell the truth about how I had fallen. My parents were furious at him for being so irresponsible. He was sent to bed without supper and without any halvah. I felt very upset and responsible that I had gotten my beloved elder brother into trouble.

*

As we grew older Esther and I became inseparable. We shared everything, including our secrets and dreams about boys. The school yard was full of boys. In the light, warm weather we arrived early in the playground to play *Cops and Robbers* with them. I was such a tom-boy that I could jump rope and double skip better than anyone else in class. But when I did handstands, or swung on the bars and somersaulted, the boys jeered they could see my bloomers, so I tried swinging one-handed to keep hold of my skirt. Of course, I lost my balance and fell heavily on to the tarmac, breaking my arm.

This time I was more frightened for Sol, who was sent for by the teacher and had to take me back to the Dairy. However, I managed to admit it was my fault before fainting away.

Papa carried me to the dispensary where they set my arm and put it in a plaster. For a while after that everyone cooed over me.

*

By the time I was ten, Sol had nearly attained the age of Barmitzvah. He was a real American boy, not at all steeped in the Hebraic traditions that supported Papa. To our father, Barmitzvah was a natural event. Every Saturday some boy or other attained manhood at the age of thirteen and was called up to read a portion of the Torah in front of the congregation. Mama was preparing to make a special Kiddush at home, but there was to be no huge celebration.

One fine spring evening, as we sat swinging on the hammock, Sol confided in me.

'If I have to have a Barmitzvah, then I suppose I must. Learning Hebrew is a drag and I don't much care for praying every morning either.'

'I wish I was a boy,' I said enviously during one of my religious bouts. 'Then I could wear a prayer shawl and sing in the choir on Shabbat.'

'Count yourself lucky,' Sol said. 'I am not looking forward to June.'

Mama overheard as she stepped onto the porch.

'Oh, I am!' she said excitedly. 'Your grandparents will be here for the Barmitzvah.'

'We know,' I said. 'They're here every weekend.'

Mama seemed oblivious of everything except the letter in her hand, which she waved at us.

'They're coming! Your father has got them out.' She beamed, and then wiped a tear from her eye.

We suddenly realised she was talking of the Meltzer family. She had not seen her parents since the day she had left Russia. My father's persuasive powers, plus his financial support, meant that he had organised Mama's dearest wish. Her mother would sit alongside her in the synagogue and her father would be called to the Bimah, the raised platform where he would read a portion of the Law at Sol's Barmitzvah.

From that moment the whole household was turned upside down in readiness. The main bedroom was to be given over to the honoured guests. My parents moved into a smaller front bedroom, leaving my older sisters to squeeze in together. Esther and I were left in peace in our tiny, cosy room. Only Sol had the privilege of sleeping on his own.

At last, Grandmother Lesha, whom we called Bubeh, and Grandpa Isaac, whom we called Zedeh, arrived speaking only Russian, Yiddish and Hebrew.

Bubeh was a small, blonde, blue-eyed lady. A real character who had raised eight children and was once more in her element looking after a large, growing family. She and Mama happily conversed in the kitchen while they prepared borscht, a Russian soup made with beetroots. This was delicious eaten cold with sour cream and diced cucumbers, or served hot with boiled potatoes.

When Bubeh offered to bake the weekly bread, as she had always done in Russia, her daughter pointed out that in the States you ordered your bread which was delivered right to your door. People came from all over to buy bread from Ticotsky's bakery, particularly their freshly baked pumpernickel for which they were famous. They also baked Vienna loaves like French bread, rye bread with hundreds of seeds, crispy white rolls for breakfast and round white schishel bread, deliciously crusty with floured bases. On Thursdays and Fridays large plaited cholas covered with poppy seeds were baked for the Sabbath. Bubeh raised her hands to heaven at the choice.

Zedeh was a tall, imperious man, sporting a neat black beard. He spoke to us in Yiddish, with great hand gestures. We knew exactly what he meant even if we did not understand a word. He was an elderly, learned Jew but very demanding, managing to keep his little wife running around after him. He had been used to being boss of a large cigarette factory and to having wealth and workers. Now he seemed lost in the New World where he was no longer master in his own house, even though Papa deferred to him and gave him head of the table. He became moody and taciturn, rarely speaking. He would spend hours out walking around the town alone.

One midwinter day Zedeh returned with a fresh hot-house cucumber. We watched as he unwrapped it carefully, cut himself a slice which he crunched loudly, after which he wrapped it up and put the rest away in his pocket.

'I wish I had some!' I complained to Mama later. But she stopped me by saying, 'He has to have something of his own to enjoy.'

On the morning of Sol's Barmitzvah, we girls helped lay the table for Kiddush, then walked to synagogue wearing our best clothes and hats. The men were already well into the service. Women sat separately at the back. First, my father was called up by the Rabbi to read from the Torah, after which Zedeh was called up. Then it was Sol's turn. He walked up to the Bimah looking very small and nervous. Zedeh and Papa stood either side of him. When Sol finished singing his portion aloud to the congregation, he heaved an enormous sigh and grinned over to me.

Then the Haftorah, sayings from the Prophets, was to be read. Zedeh spoke quietly to the Rabbi, who nodded. We waited as Zedeh carefully replaced his spectacles on his nose, took his stand with the book and started to sing. We were enthralled as his magnificent voice filled the building. The whole congregation murmured approval and shouted '*Shecoyach!*' (strength!) as he stepped down from the Bimah, many coming forward to shake his hand. From that day on he became the cantor in the synagogue. He had found his home.

Soon afterwards we were taken to see Al Jolson in the first talking picture *'The Jazz Singer'*, where Jolson sang in the synagogue, just like our grandfather. We were thrilled to pieces.

Eventually I made it through Sixth Grade to follow my older sisters and brother into Troupe Junior High School. Esther must have felt left out because I began to act more like a grown-up, especially now I could wear hand-downs from my older sisters. I was a teenager now, a person with views and ability, equal to anyone, even my parents. One morning, I came upon my father walking down the stairs towards me.

'Hello J.L!' I greeted him cheekily.

He stopped and looked down at me, considering my bluff.

'Hello!' He smiled. 'You can call me anything you like, but *never* refer to me as your old man.'

'Okay!' I tossed my hair and went out through the front door thinking, '*Well, if he doesn't care that I call him J.L., then what's the point?*'

I always called him *Papa* after that.

CHAPTER 4

Troupe Junior High (1932 – 1933)

By the time I was fifteen and at Troupe Junior High, my older sisters were settled into their careers. Rhea trained as a nurse in the Brooklyn Jewish Hospital, where she now lived and worked. She was engaged to marry one of the doctors there. Leah was a dental hygienist who trained at the Forsyth Dental School in Boston. She lived at home and worked for the New Haven health department. Rose, who also lived at home, was a qualified teacher employed in the local school system.

We three youngsters, Sol, Esther and I, were still carefree. We enjoyed everything life had to offer to energetic American kids. At school I was having the time of my life as a social bug. I was extremely popular, always in demand. I realised it was not for myself but for my connections. Girls were like flies around a honey-pot where handsome boys were concerned and I had two of them right there in my family. When friends introduced me they would say, 'Do you know Harriett? She's Sol Gold's sister.'

Sure, I had a good-looking brother and an even better looking cousin, Joe Gold, whom I adored. Every girl wanted to have them at their parties so I was always asked along in the hope that my relatives would come as my escorts. I knew that! But I accepted all invitations willingly and my friends were often lucky. Sol or Joe usually did accompany me.

However, after accepting one party invitation for Saturday night from a classmate, I was really shocked when my parents pronounced 'No way!'

'Why? She's my school friend, Lillian. What's wrong with her?' I demanded.

'Look, greet everybody as a friend,' explained Papa. 'But who you ask home is an entirely different matter. Never accept an invitation unless you know you can ask them back to your house. And in this case, you can't.'

I had no idea what Lillian or her family had done to antagonise Papa but he stuck to the rule and absolutely forbade me to leave the house. I was mad because everyone else was going out that Saturday and I was left at home alone. I fumed and fretted around like a trapped bird until I suddenly remembered that one of my older sisters had left a copy of the infamous life of the Marquis de Sade hidden under her bed. I searched under her mattress until I found it, then flounced downstairs, flung myself on to the settee and read it from cover to cover. When I put it back in its hiding place I had hardly understood one word, but I felt immense satisfaction that I was paying my parents back.

That year Sol was about to graduate from High School. It brought home to me the need to work hard to gain good grades. No particular career beckoned me. I had not mapped out my future at all, but I was particularly good at English and languages. I knew these were subjects in which I could excel, especially since Miss Norton, our English teacher, positively inspired her classes. She had the knack of a great teacher in explaining everything clearly. I still recall the thrill of the *Tale of the Ancient Mariner*, which I learnt entirely by heart from beginning to end. The words *Water, water everywhere and all the boards did shrink; Water, water everywhere, nor any drop to drink* stuck in my mind every time

I opened the fridge door to help myself to a bottle of cool water.

One unbearably hot day I raced home from school with that idea in mind. I opened the Fridgidaire, grabbed a bottle from the shelf and gulped down a sour, biting mouthful of white acid. My screams sent Mama running in. She gasped at my grimaces while the acid scorched my mouth and throat. She quickly pulled me over to the sink and washed out my mouth with tap water, insisting that I drink glass after glass of water afterwards. It was an accident, no one got into trouble and no real harm was done. But my mother admonished me saying, 'You are so impetuous, Harriett. Just learn to think before you act.'

I did not think I was impetuous. In particular, I was very reticent with boys, although I did fancy one or two. Jack was a tall, blond good-looker, who always seemed to saunter past our house just when I sat on the hammock, swinging my long dangling legs.

'Just passing!' he grinned, ambling over.

He was so tall he could stand with one foot on the ground and one on the porch while he nonchalantly made conversation. I thought he was terrific. I knew he knew I existed! That thrilled me to pieces.

'Going to the baseball match?' he asked. 'Your brother is a great catcher!'

It was usually my brothers or sisters who were praised, rarely myself.

'You are a real smart-aleck,' he teased. 'You gained the prize in English this semester, didn't you?'

'Oh, that wasn't much.' I shrugged, secretly pleased that I had impressed him. 'My cousin Joe wins every prize going!'

We eventually got to sitting next to each other on the steps of the porch, but he never plucked up courage to ask me out and I was never that forward.

Then another tall, good-looking boy, Abe, caught my eye. On my way to school, I deliberately took the turning past his house especially to bump into him accidentally on purpose. I had a real crush on him, but we never got farther than smart conversation.

In any case, life was great. I was in no hurry to pick a partner, although I expected to be married by the time I was twenty one.

Despite all the financial problems during the recession, father's business thrived.

'Look ahead. Modernisation is the thing,' he said as he added improvements to his dairy business.

Everybody accepted change as the norm. We took new inventions in our stride. Our telephone, once an upright with a separate ear-piece, was now a modern looking instrument with ear and talk piece together. We girls used it extensively to arrange our social life.

We felt very modern as we pulled our chairs around the radio in the sitting room to listen to Eddie Cantor, or concert music, or the news. In the cinema, the movies were enticing us into another world of romance and rhapsody.

Automobiles became more reliable and, as Mr. Ford said, we could have any colour we liked as long as it was black. When Lindbergh had flown the Atlantic in May 1927, not a great deal of the world beyond Connecticut had seeped into our consciousness. Nowadays flight was possible.

'One day, maybe not in my lifetime, you will take an aeroplane and arrive in Europe in no time,' predicted J.L.

Several of my friends had already travelled abroad on large ocean liners. One of them had recently returned from

Palestine, which he delighted to describe to us in graphic detail. The unbearable heat, the sand, the flies, the stench, we could not imagine. He had hated it. I gritted my teeth and vowed it was one place I would never visit.

One afternoon, when I was in the school corridor doing my monitor's job, I heard from the street below the paperboy shouting 'Extra! Extra! Lindbergh baby kidnapped!'

I burst into the classroom interrupting lessons to tell everybody. Miss Norton stopped me in my tracks with a look, but she and the rest of the class gasped that such an awful thing could happen to our hero. It sent a gloom over everyone. Progress seemed to be accompanied by pain.

Later in the year, during the winter vacation, I was in the kitchen helping Mama prepare a festival meal for Chanukah.

'Your father is thinking of selling the business,' she remarked quietly.

'Why?' I was astonished.

'It's getting too much for Papa. Besides he has other ideas.' She looked pensive.

'What ideas?' My heart began to sink.

'Let him tell you himself.'

That evening after we had lit the first tiny candle with the shamash and sung *Maoz Tsur* together, he announced his intentions.

'Next April we are going to live in Palestine.' He was emphatic and nodded to our mother who smiled serenely, but said nothing.

I was stunned. I heard myself burst out, 'I'm not going anywhere! I'm an American. I'm not going to that God-forsaken place!'

'You are coming with us,' Papa insisted. 'And no-one calls the Holy Land God-forsaken.'

'Foreign, fly-infested and swampy!' I retorted, turning red with fury.

How could he even think of uprooting me from the place where I belonged? Where all my friends were, where my schooling was, where my future lay before me, secure and inviting.

'I will stay here with Leah, Rhea and Rose,' I said, appealing to my older sisters who did not look too keen to look after me. All the while Sol and Esther sat miserably, saying nothing.

That night I lay in bed resolved to go my own way. There were plenty of family members around. Bubeh and Zeder had recently acquired an apartment of their own nearby. Couldn't I stay to look after them?

After a fitful night, I awoke in the early hours determined to organise my own life. Esther lay in bed watching me pack a few clothes into a holdall. I put my fingers to her lips. Then I crept downstairs, let myself out of the house and made my way to cousin Joe's home.

My aunt and uncle must have known of Papa's plans because they were not too surprised to see me standing on their doorstep first thing in the morning, bag in hand.

'May I come and live with you?' I pleaded. 'I'll work for you now in the holidays and help in the business after I graduate. Anything, except leave America.'

Cousin Joe appeared in the hallway and put his arms around me as I burst into tears. That seemed to encourage them to agree. Before long they had cheerfully supplied me with a white apron and put me behind their dairy shop counter. At the end of a couple of days I had earned real money of my own and was confident I was set up for life. I felt elated.

My parents left me in this false paradise for a time until they turned up in the shop one morning expressing great surprise to see me behind the counter. I waited for the explosion.

'What is it you want, Harriett?' asked my father quietly.

'I don't want to go with you. I'll stay and work here.' Nothing was going to dissuade me.

My mother's lips trembled as J.L. came behind the counter and led me into the back of the shop.

'Look, I'll make a deal with you,' he said. 'If you go with an open mind and after a year you don't like it, no-one will stop you returning to the States.'

I remained silent.

'Are you going to miss such an opportunity to see the world?' he coaxed. 'A tour of the Mediterranean is one most girls of your age would give anything for.' He paused. There were tears in his eyes. 'I realise that this is my dream, Harriett, but you are part of it. Believe me, you won't regret coming with us.'

'But what about college and my education?' I said.

'I will tell you. One must read, one must learn and study – but finally one must *experience* to understand fully. This will be a wonderful experience for you. What can you lose? A year out of the States? Then you can come back and work in the shop for the rest of your life, if you want that.'

I may have been a typical American teenage kid, but I was not stupid. Maybe I was just sixteen, but I could see a good offer when it came. Papa had persuaded me and I accepted with alacrity.

'Okay, one condition.' I did not want to surrender too easily now that I had gotten the taste for earning money.

'Can I work here in my spare time until we go?'

So it was all agreed.

But the thought of leaving the States still nagged at me and I remained in two minds. The roots of my world were being torn up. I could not help being resentful and complained loudly to my friends at school. Miss Gallagher, who was our Ancient History teacher, overheard me and came over.

When I told her why I was so angry, she exclaimed, 'Aren't you lucky!' Was I? I did not understand why.

That afternoon, Miss Gallagher addressed the class.

'I am going to arrange to bring the next semester of work forward especially for Harriett. We're going to learn about ancient Greece, Babylon, the Euphrates, the Tigris and all the wonderful history surrounding Palestine. And if Harriett doesn't want to go after that, I'll give up teaching!'

She was divinely inspired. Miss Gallagher's lessons were so amazing that my imagination was caught with stories of that part of the world. I became utterly intrigued with the whole idea, even though I was reluctant to admit it to anyone. At last, in my heart, I began to feel that everything was going to be all right.

From Troupe Junior High School I moved on to Hillhouse High School to finish my education whilst awaiting our departure from the United States.

The whole of New Haven seemed to know of the Gold family's plans to emigrate to Palestine. Many people were puzzled that we should wish to leave the good life to follow a dream. Others looked upon us as pioneers working for all Jews. Dozens of farewell parties were organised for us. We embarked on a non-stop round of dinner and dancing parties. Every occasion was an emotional farewell. We were saying goodbye to the past whilst being uncertain of our future. But strangely, there were no regrets. I began to realise that I was very privileged and courageous setting off on an unknown adventure with J.L., visionary and pioneer.

CHAPTER 5

SS Vulcania (1934)

Before the end of February 1934 my father had realised his assets. The dairy, shops and my childhood home had all been sold. We went out on numerous shopping expeditions for every conceivable item of clothing. Our trunks for the voyage were packed with New Haven's most fashionable garments. Furniture and precious items from our home were crated for embarkation whilst we awaited the final date of departure in early April.

In order that Leah and Rose might be well set up in New Haven, my parents had bought them an apartment in a beautiful old stone house. In the meantime, before emigration, we all stayed comfortably with them. An up-to-date oil heating system kept us cosy during the dark winter days leaving the huge decorative stone fireplaces empty with alcoves filled with baskets of logs just for show.

'Dusting will soon be a thing of the past, in the States at any rate,' said our mother, patting a radiator.

Spring was coming. By now it was well into March, but the weather suddenly turned bitterly cold. On our way back from school, north winds nipped our ears as Esther and I discussed the idea of moving to a different climate.

'Swimming every day,' said Esther, remembering hot summer holidays.

'Flies and bugs everywhere!' I added, remembering what I had heard about Palestine.

The following morning we awoke to a freezing apartment. The windows were frosted over. When I rubbed a peep-hole to look outside, everything was covered with a layer of smooth white snow. Nothing was moving, only the muffled silence that deep snow brings to a city.

Neither Leah nor Rose could think of getting to work and both were grumbling that the oil delivery, which was due that day, would never be able to arrive. We were out of oil and out of heat.

'So much for modernity,' said Mama turning to J.L. 'Please do something!'

Under J.L.'s instructions we helped tear up newspapers which we stuffed into various grates. We soon had logs roaring on the open fires. Apart from our old basement boiler, I could not remember having seen an open fire before. I sat watching the flames catch, flicker high and radiate into a spread of brightness and warmth.

Sol and I insisted on going outside. We wrapped up in as many layers as possible and stumbled down the front steps, screaming with laughter as we found ourselves sinking knee high into deep snow. The only traffic we could see was a milk float several blocks away stuck in a bank of snow.

'Let's help!' I suggested, as we waded our way along the sidewalk.

'Just like old times,' laughed Sol, as we helped deliver pints of milk and groceries.

'Thank goodness we're leaving for a hot country,' I said and meant it.

That year we celebrated Seder night for the Passover in the home of friends. The large gathering around the table wished us well. After the service and blessings, when we said 'Next year in Jerusalem!', everyone cheered. My heart leapt. Papa's dream was becoming a reality.

*

The SS Vulcania was docked in New York harbour awaiting our arrival. All who embarked could be seen off by friends or relatives. We had said farewell to Bubeh and Zedeh in New Haven. It must have been hard for them to lose their daughter yet again to another country.

My stomach was dealing with butterflies as we boarded the huge ship. Esther and I were shown to a second-class cabin by a smartly uniformed steward, who saluted as he ushered us inside. We fell giggling into the cabin. I opened the wardrobe and stared into the mirror on the door. An elegant young lady wearing a pert little green hat and matching suit stared back. I was wearing my first truly adult outfit and I looked good in it. I suddenly realised that this was not only a journey into a new land and a new beginning, I was leaving my childhood behind.

Esther, wearing a neat brown suit, flung herself onto the bunk and sniffed back tears. It had not occurred to me that she might also be feeling apprehensive or miserable leaving America.

'Come along, we're going to have the time of our lives,' I comforted her. 'We don't have to dress up first night out, then tomorrow we can enjoy the voyage. Let's go and find the others.'

J.L.'s parents had accompanied us to New York harbour and were now sitting in our main cabin waiting to say farewell. Various aunts, uncles, cousins and friends moved in and out all afternoon. We were inundated with bouquets and telegrams. One of them was addressed to me. It read: 'Don't catch any poor fish with that line of yours!' I laughed. It was from our friends, the Barnetts, who evidently thought I had what it took to keep men hooked.

Everybody we loved came to wish us well in the flower-filled cabin. Drinks flowed freely as we were toasted on our way. Leah and Rose had driven with us to New York. Eventually Rhea arrived with her fiancé. In one corner Mama stood quietly talking to the daughters she was leaving behind. It was more of a wrench for her than anyone. But she had left her parents before and seen them come to live nearby again. Who knew what the future held?

There were warm embraces as the ship's bell rang: 'All ashore those going ashore!'

The passengers indulged in final kisses, hugs and handshakes.

'Don't forget to write! Send me your new address!'

'The middle of nowhere, Desert Land, Palestine,' I thought dryly.

I hugged my elder sisters tightly.

'I'll be back next year,' I whispered to Rose. 'You can count on it.'

Everyone went on deck to watch the guests disembark, madly waving handkerchiefs and scarves as they looked back at us. Below, small boats hooted farewell while the crowds on the quayside cheered, waved flags and threw balloons in the air. As the great ship pulled away her deep siren sounded in reply. We bade farewell to the Statue of Liberty as we moved sedately and surely out of the East river into the open sea.

That evening, Esther and I joined our parents and Sol for dinner in the elegant dining-room with candelabra on every table. The ship had a fully kosher dining room in addition to the others, so we were content to browse through a huge printed menu offering dozens of delicacies. It took me a while to decide what to eat. I need not have bothered.

Within hours of sailing I began to feel terribly ill. My head swam, my stomach heaved and I lay prostrate on my bunk with a wet towel on my forehead groaning that I wanted to die. Esther fetched mother, who told me briskly that it was only seasickness and that I would recover in no time, but I did not believe her.

The following lunchtime Esther came into the cabin with a plate of food.

'Take it away,' I moaned.

'Mama says to eat pickled cucumbers - it will settle your stomach.'

I hardly believed her but I sucked one, nibbled a bit and astonishingly began to feel better.

'It's a strange medicine,' I said when mother came in to see how I was.

'I remember it worked for me,' she chuckled. 'All those years ago.'

By the third day out, with the weather fair, the sun glorious, I had recovered enough to take my promenade on deck. Other youngsters, many of whom were emigrating as well, were enjoying the air, playing quoits and deck tennis. I sank into a deckchair to watch them.

'Hi! Harriett!' A tall, debonair young man raised his cap to me.

'Jack! It is so good to see a familiar face. Whatever are you doing on board?'

'Going to work.' He grinned down at me. 'I graduated as an architect last year. No better work than building a homeland in Palestine.'

'That is what it is all about,' said Papa, coming to sit beside me.

The luxurious cruise lasted four weeks. Every night we put on evening dress for dinner in the kosher dining-room. A waiter brought over the wine list and deferentially handed it to my father. J.L. ordered mineral water for us and wine for himself and mother.

'Never drink alcohol out of home,' he said, seeing my face.

'Why?' I thought he was being mean.

'As soon as you have a drink, you are another person. That new person needs a drink and that makes you another person - and so on. My advice is don't have the first drink and stay who you are!'

'I can understand that,' I said. 'But not even a little wine?'

'So long as you see who pours it,' he said relenting, pouring me half a glass of white wine. 'If anyone offers you a drink, never take it if you have not seen it poured.' He waggled his finger at me. 'It could be a Mickey Finn.'

After dinner we rose to join other passengers in the ballroom, ready to dance into the small hours.

'I am having a fabulous time living in luxury,' I said to Sol as he accompanied me up the staircase.

'Let's sneak up to First Class,' he said, ushering me up another flight of stairs to the First Class ballroom.

'Don't get lost,' called mother.

'We're on a ship!' exclaimed Sol to me. 'I want to explore every part of it.'

But we soon discovered something very peculiar. Those rich passengers were really old and fuddy-duddy. All the youngsters from First Class were coming down to our deck because we were having much more fun. So we just turned around and joined them.

It was like entering a dream world. Junior naval officers dressed in smart, white uniforms, had been instructed to look after young women passengers to keep them happy. I was happy! I noticed three gorgeous men elbow each other across the dance floor to get to *me* first. Stunning, handsome men were actually vying with each other to dance with *me*. I did not much care who won the race, so long as I was dancing.

'Do you come here often?' teased the officer.

I blushed. I had always thought other people smarter than I and still found it difficult to converse with a stranger.

'Don't you know you are an extremely pretty girl?' he continued.

I was in his arms, swaying to the music. It was enough to make a girl lose her heart.

'You are blonde, blue eyed, tall and willowy. Just what a chap likes.'

His arm tightened around my waist. I stiffened. Even I knew a line when I heard one. In any case, I was conditioned to understand that non-Jewish men were not part of my world. They would court a pretty girl, but never marry her. It was all just fun.

Nevertheless, since none of my dancing partners knew my background or my parents, I realised they liked me for myself alone. Suddenly I was no longer an American jazz-age kid, member of the large extended Gold family. I was Harriett Gold in my own right.

*

SS Vulcania stopped at Gibraltar, where we visited the apes. The ship then sailed to Palma de Mallorca, where we disembarked for a day's tour. The weather was bright and balmy. We walked around the narrow winding streets of the old city, shaded and enclosed, peering into darkened shops. Small, sun-tanned children stood watching us from doorways. Mallorcans smiled and welcomed us, but there was an air of poverty and decay around the old buildings. A smell of olive oil and humanity pervaded the air. People spoke a mixture of Spanish and French and I caught the odd word that I understood. It was the first time I had set foot in a land where English was not the native tongue.

Our next stop was Nice. From there we voyaged to Naples, where we ascended the hills that overlooked the bay. Here we were given refreshments before being coached to Pompeii. I could hardly contain myself. Stone-like figures that had once been human evoked in me an enormous awe. The remains of a vibrant Roman town with wall paintings depicting those ancient times, together with the story of the eruption of Vesuvius in AD. 79, imbued in me a great respect for this lost civilisation. After this it seemed facile to be occupied with who was wearing what or which party I was going to join that evening.

The ship visited Palermo, from where we sailed to Piraeus, Greece, and docked for two days. Our family decided to take the train into Athens. Tours to the Acropolis, which rose magnificently above us, cost over five dollars a person. Father felt that fifteen dollars was more than enough to pay so he and mother remained behind whilst Esther, Sol and I took the tour.

The architecture took my breath away, such magnificent buildings. We entered the Parthenon, temple of Athena, Goddess of Wisdom. We wondered at the sacred olive tree. We looked down over Athens, the seat of democracy. I was overwhelmed. Miss Gallagher had done her work well. I became aware that I was a thinking person in that big wide world beyond New Haven.

*

4th May 1934.

Esther and I were awakened by father early in the morning

'It's 6.am. Come up on deck. We are entering the bay of Haifa,' he said, his voice choking with emotion.

On deck we joined many excited passengers. In the dawn light of spring, Haifa was a sight to behold. With the green hills of Carmel rising against the background of a clear bright sky, the white buildings were bathed in a translucent glow. The Mediterranean shimmered in the early light as our huge ship steamed sedately towards the harbour.

Here we waited for what seemed hours to be manoeuvred into dock. Looking down from the great height of the deck, the quayside appeared almost insignificant. Tiny figures below, Arabs in white robes, moved around stacking crates and shifting cargo. British soldiers in khaki shouted commands. A reception crowd of Jews waved and beamed up at us. I turned to J.L. who was standing behind me. He placed his hand on my shoulder.

'This is a dream,' I said, feeling the aura of the East.

Finally the gangways were lowered. With a last glance at our cabin, Esther and I gathered our belongings and disembarked with our family, while Arab porters carried the larger luggage behind us. A smell of oil and sea arose in the fresh warm air. All around us there was the impression of activity and industry as we stood in queues waiting to be admitted.

Immigration control seemed to take forever. Sol had his own passport. Esther and I were included in J.L's because we were under eighteen. We stood beside our parents as British officers carefully examined our passports, visas, papers, until eventually they indicated we were free to enter Palestine.

As we strode out beyond the customs buildings, J.L. knelt down and kissed the ground.

CHAPTER 6

Palestine (May-August 1934)

Up to the moment of my arrival in Palestine I had no idea what to expect. The first thing I realised was that there was a British High Commissioner in control, Sir Arthur Wauchope. We had come as immigrants, so were considered to be aliens by the British. My father held three certificates of entry which he had bought for a large sum; one for himself, one for my mother and one for Sol. Esther and I were exempt since we were under eighteen.

J.L. excelled as a traveller and was very knowledgeable. He spoke four languages, Russian, English, Yiddish and Hebrew (although his accent was different) so he easily made himself understood. Firstly, he organised our luggage to be forwarded to the hotel. Then he turned to us and beamed.

'The first thing to see is Mount Carmel,' he said.

It had rained overnight. Now the sun was shining, making the area lush and green. The land appeared beautifully inviting. So much excitement!

I had been expecting dirt and flies everywhere. Instead there were paved streets, modern houses, small, neat blocks of flats and shops. As we walked on Mount Carmel, the higher we climbed the grander were the houses overlooking the bay. All road signs were shown in three languages, English, Arabic and Hebrew.

'Some translations are very odd,' laughed Sol, pointing to a shop sign which read *'Please enter sideways.'*

We skirted around a group of children playing hopscotch in the street, chattering away to each other in Hebrew.

'Aren't they clever speaking Hebrew like that!' exclaimed Esther.

'You're clever too,' said J.L. 'You can speak English fluently. Hebrew is their native tongue.'

Until then we had not thought of Hebrew, the language of prayer, as a living language. This was the first inkling that here was another country, another people to whom we related. Here were Jewish people like us, with kids speaking everyday Hebrew. It gave me a real thrill.

Later in the day we arrived at our hotel in Tel Aviv. Having been on a very luxurious ship, it seemed rather small, but we took everything in our stride.

'I must have a shower,' I exclaimed as I flopped on to my bed.

'Let's hope the plumbing is okay,' warned Esther.

To our surprise Tel Aviv was extremely modern. The facilities were much better than some of the places we had visited on the Continent where we had had to use a hole in the ground. We rested on our beds listening to the noises of the city as the heat of the afternoon cooled towards evening.

Before too long J.L. knocked on our door.

'I'm taking you to meet a friend I knew back in Russia. We were both Zionists, both idealists. He left for South Africa when I went to the States. We made a pact - but Braude got here first!'

With the sound of music emanating from nearby cafes, we followed J.L.'s fast pace down Montefiore Street into Allenby Street, then right into Bialek Street, until we stopped before a grand house. We waited as he knocked on the door. When it opened his old friend held out his arms to us and these two gentlemen, in tears, embraced on the doorstep.

'Come in! Let me introduce you to my wife and my children,' said Mr. Braude, juggling us around so that everyone was introduced to everyone else.

We youngsters soon moved to one side to talk. I was drawn immediately to their daughter, Phyllis, who was a slender brunette, full of vitality and fun.

'Hello, it is really good to meet you. When did you arrive?' she asked with her South African accent.

'We've only just come off the boat!' I exclaimed. 'I can hardly get my bearings.'

'We arrived twelve weeks ago and rented this lovely house. It is thrilling to be in Palestine, isn't it? My father has dreamed about it for years.'

'So has mine,' I said as we laughed together.

'It does not take long to settle in. I'll show you around if you like.'

She was naturally outgoing and friendly. I was still only sixteen, so Phyllis at almost eighteen seemed very sophisticated, a real smart gal. I secretly felt that if I could be like her and lose all my shyness I would be confident of my opinions.

Within half an hour we youngsters decided to go out to a nearby cafe. Throughout our voyage I had imagined I was going into a wilderness, but boy, had I been wrong! Tel Aviv was a civilised built-up city. I could hardly contain myself as we excused ourselves from our parents and left them to their memories. Phyllis and her friend, Bill, met up outside with one or two other acquaintances before we pushed through the doors of a cafe in Allenby Street. All I needed was jazz and dancing, and here it was - a dance floor with a jazz band playing *Alexander's Ragtime Band*. One of Bill's friends immediately took me by the waist and stepped me out to the music. I was exhilarated. Life had started!

It was well past eleven when Sol and I walked back in the warm night air to our hotel. Esther was already sound asleep. I lay down in a dream, recalling all that I would write in my letters back home.

Next morning Mother woke us up. Even though it was early, the day already felt hot and humid.

'We're going visiting,' she said. 'Dress in something light.'

We were taken to visit her cousin, Gissa, who had emigrated years before from St. Petersburg. She was a Meltzer, as was mother in her single days. Now married to an engineer, she was an eminent dental surgeon. Mama and Gissa embraced tearfully in her smart, spacious apartment, speaking rapid Russian to each other and catching up on the lost years. Esther, Sol and I made friends with our newly found cousins, who were near enough our age to give us something in common. It was strange to meet family so far from home.

The whole week was reunion time for my parents. Rose and Sam Levine from Chattanooga, USA, who had done Zionist work with J.L., welcomed us with delight. Another family from New Haven who had lived across the street from us, (oddly enough, I never remembered being particularly friendly with them in the States), invited us to stay with them on the Sabbath. We enjoyed a Friday night meal in their home, slept there overnight and accompanied them to synagogue on Saturday morning. They and their children made us feel very welcome, but they were more religious than anyone I had known before. They had their toilet paper torn up, ready for use on the Sabbath. Can you imagine that?

I had not been expecting to enjoy the company of other young Americans in my first weeks away from New Haven, but here I was 'back in civilisation'. That is, I thought I was until the British radio station reported that police were still looking for the murderers of two Jewish men who had been found shot on the Tel Aviv sea front. Everyone was concerned. Were they shot by Arabs or the British, or perhaps even other Jews? They were known to be right wing, hardy Zionists who were determined to regain Palestine as a Jewish State. There was an underlying current of suspicion and fear manifesting itself in this new city. The news had spread quickly and their murderers were still at large. The mystery was unlikely to be solved, and it became apparent that there was an underground organisation that everyone knew of but kept silent about. I did not like to ask too many questions.

On the other hand, everyone wanted to know about me.

'Are you going to settle here ?' was the main question.

'My parents are,' I replied.

'Where?'

'We're going to live in Herzlia, Azor Gimmel - Zone Three.'

'Oh, out in the sand dunes,' they said. 'Patrolled by guards on horseback.'

'Why do we need guarding? We won't do anything wrong!' I exclaimed, completely ignorant of the need for protection.

*

We left Tel Aviv by bus early in the morning to arrive at Herzlia before noon. It was a very small town surrounded by orange groves and peopled by American families who had emigrated to Palestine before us. We took a taxi one and a half miles further on to a tiny hamlet near to an Arab village.

The sun was at its zenith when we tumbled out of the cab and into Mrs. Mandelbaum's spacious house. It was built in the style of an American colonial house with a pitched roof, one of a few homes built on a hill overlooking the orange groves. Here, for the time being, J.L. had rented two bedrooms, sharing the kitchen and living rooms.

A track road ran down to the groves past a house built into the side of the hill. We found out later that it belonged to the Shuchmans, who had turned their basement into a grocery store, supplying all the immediate needs of the growing community. The whole area ran in stages of development by immigrant families who had bought plots of sand years before. Some newcomers were Russians or Poles but the majority, like Mrs. Mandelbaum, were from the States. In the house next door lived Mr. and Mrs. Mabowitz whose daughter, Golda, was an ardent Zionist. She eventually became Golda Meir, the Prime Minister of Israel.

Mrs. Mandelbaum was a vital little lady, with black wiry hair which looked as if it had been *marcelled*. She let rooms in her home to newcomers and cooked meals for people to eat in her house, which was bustling with builders and visitors. She had three sons, so Sol hung around with them when he was not helping father.

The boys did not interest me at all. Nor did the daily tasks that occupied Mother. Somehow, she managed to cook using a Primus stove with paraffin in the base. It had to be pumped up, then lit. It would burst into a huge flame which eventually died down to a steady glow. No matter how sweltering the weather was, Mama always managed to give us a hot daily meal. She seemed determined to keep our life as stable as possible.

I left Esther to her own devices and wandered around to make my own friends. In the room next door I came across a pretty young woman, barely older than twenty, sitting on the bed. I hesitated at the open door.

'Hi! I'm Harriett. Can I come in?'

'Sure. It's hot, isn't it?' She beckoned me inside. 'I'm Devora Segal. My parents own the grocery store down the hill. Good to meet you.' She stretched her legs along the sheet and wiped her forehead. 'I'm glad to have company. I can't go far. I'm expecting.'

'Can I get you anything?' I did not know whether I should be concerned or not.

'No, really. I'm contented, truly. Hymie, my husband will be back soon.' Her face lit up as she spoke of him. 'Only another ten weeks.' She patted her stomach and laughed. 'We've been married seven months and soon we will be three. Come and talk to me, tell me all about yourself.'

I had always thought other people were much smarter than I. That I was gawky, ungainly and not at all good looking. But during the past weeks I had begun a whole new appraisal of myself. The Harriett Ida Gold who emerged was no longer a member of a large extended family, no longer daughter of 'Gold's Dairy', nor younger sister of elegant siblings. In that, my father had been right. The journey to Palestine had been much more than a voyage of discovery. It had liberated me to think for myself, to have confidence in my own opinions, to begin to know my own worth. To my surprise, I suddenly realised that I had grown up.

*

In that first week, J.L. set about planning a house with a flat roof on his piece of land. Jack, the architect I had met on ship, arrived to supervise the work. In the meantime, Sol, Esther and I made for the sea shore. We walked along the dunes beside the orange groves towards the echoes of our summer holidays in the States. We were well aware of the discipline of the sea. We had owned rafts, canoes, even boats in the States.

We raced over the hot sands and plunged into the Mediterranean, losing ourselves in the joy of swimming and fooling around in the cool, salt water. By the time we had had enough, I felt my back stinging.

'You're awfully red,' remarked Esther, whose dark, olive skin browned safely. She helped me pull my summer dress over my costume. My back smarted.

'Put a towel around your shoulders,' advised Sol. 'Better still, put it over your head on the way home.'

I stumbled back in a daze and flopped on to the bed. My back felt red raw. I had a raging thirst and soon became delirious with sun-stroke. People drifted in and out of the room and my consciousness. I could hear myself moaning. Mother came to feed me tenderly with fluids as I lay on my stomach, gradually recovering. Over the next ten days the skin which had peeled off my back began to heal.

'Now you know how vicious the sun can be,' Mama said, when I was feeling more myself. 'Things out here may seem the same as the States - but they are far more dangerous. From now on, take more care.'

J.L. came to see how I was and gave me another lecture.

'Never go down to the beach on your own again,' he warned.

'I was with Sol and Esther,' I protested.

'That's not enough. There's safety in numbers,' he insisted. 'Not everyone around here is glad to see immigrants. Not everyone is used to lithe females uncovered from head to toe throwing themselves about in the water. Remember, there are other cultures out here that think what you do is far from moral.' He winked at me. 'I know that you would not do anything immoral, but our ways are not always understood by the Arabs. Be aware of the danger and take care.'

I promised, not knowing that danger would come unexpectedly without my being able to do anything about it.

From then on life became a great holiday. We Golds were a contented crowd of three. Everyone wanted to make friends with us. On Saturdays all the youngsters in the place went down to the beach for the day. We gathered together to walk towards the pure unadulterated sands; one large, happy crowd of young men and women, carefree and eager for the future.

Jack, the architect, was still visiting us to oversee our building arrangements. In August, he brought along two pals who were on vacation. Although I was up and about by now feeling very fit, my knees went weak when I saw them.

'This is Sammy, late of the States.' Jack introduced me to a tall, blond gorgeous guy.

'Hi, I'm Joseph,' said his dark, handsome friend. 'But you can call me Doccy on account of.....'

'We know!' interrupted Jack and Sammy. 'You passed your medical exams.'

'*I'm spoilt for choice!*' I thought.

'Join us!' I insisted as we swept them along with a huge crowd of friends and visitors carrying picnics to the beach, singing on our way.

There were some young people already playing on the sand, cheerfully shouting to each other in a foreign language. Our crowd settled down to eat and drink, sit and watch the sea. The black flag was flying that day as a warning. We knew there was a dangerous undertow, so we only dipped our feet into the water and splashed each other. Sammy sat alongside me as I lay back under a towel dreaming which of these new guys I would like to date.

'Don't go into the water!' Sammy's yell made me sit up as a young woman and a little boy from the foreign group ran into the surf.

'They can't understand you,' I said, watching them dance out into the waves and plunge into the sea.

'Are they crazy or plain stupid!' Sol's shadow stood over me as he looked out to sea.

Almost at once we could see they were getting into trouble, probably not even aware they were going to drown. They were too busy thrashing around to cry out for help as the undercurrent caught them and pulled them around and out, carrying them away from the beach.

'We've got to get into the water to rescue them,' yelled Sol. 'Everyone, hold hands! Watch out for the undertow!'

We managed to form a human chain, hanging on to each other's hands for dear life. The shifting sands dragged away under my feet causing me to lose my balance and go under. I was tugged up again by Doccy who grabbed at me. No matter how we tried we could not reach the strangers. They were being pulled farther and farther out.

'It's too dangerous,' said Doccy eventually, guiding me back to the shore. 'Everyone come back. I'm a strong swimmer. I'll go for them.'

He dived under the waves and swam towards the bobbing heads.

Sammy yelled out, 'Push them back to me, Doccy!' and plunged in after him.

The rest of us stood knee deep in the water, watching and waiting as the two boys managed to reach the flailing arms and push the newcomers back towards us. We caught at them and dragged the two safely ashore where they lay exhausted and panting, but alive. We were all so relieved we had got them out of danger that for a while we thought of nothing else.

We waited for Sammy and Doccy to emerge from the sea to congratulate them. There was no sign of them. We called for them and cried out. But they never returned. They had been swept away, overpowered by the force of the sea.

Their bodies were carried so far out that they did not come ashore anywhere near where we had stood. Doccy's body was found after two days. Sammy's corpse was not recovered until ten days later. He had been carried along the coast for miles. Their parents came to take their bodies home.

To us they were heroes. Brave young men lost to the sea due to the ignorance and stupidity of new immigrants who had risked their own lives for fun, causing others to make the ultimate sacrifice to save them.

There was a morbidity around us. Everyone felt down. Mother comforted me by saying that life must go on. I knew that, but it did not stop me mourning for these young men, or reliving what I had felt for them.

At the end of the week, during the early hours, Devora's cries came through the walls of her room. Hymie, her husband, ran down the road to fetch her mother from the grocer's house.

'The baby's on the way!' he yelled.

I could hear moans and screams throughout the morning. Sol and the boys left the house whilst Mrs. Mandelbaum and Mother were busy, keeping things organised and calm.

At long last, around midday, we heard a baby cry, accompanied by laughter, singing and jollity coming from Devora's room.

'Mazeltov! It's a boy!' Everyone was crying with happiness. 'A Sabra! Born in the Holy land.'

CHAPTER 7

Herzlia (August 1934)

Over the past month the events of life and death had left me feeling introspective and cautious about remaining in Palestine. I needed someone to turn to. I had made friends with an American boy, Chaim, who also stayed in Herzlia. He was five years older than I, not too tall but with smiling eyes and a ready grin. Often he took turns to patrol our small settlement with a gun slung over his shoulder, as did all young men organised to keep an eye out for any Arab attack. He was someone outside my family to whom I could talk about my reservations.

'I'm not staying after my year is up,' I told Chaim, who knew about the deal my father had made with me.

We were strolling down towards the orchard grove in the cooling air of evening. Chaim was thoughtful.

'I came because I wanted to. No one needed to persuade me,' he said. 'In fact, my parents keep pressing me to go back to the States.'

'Will you go?'

'Not if I can help it. I'm part of the Haganah, looking after you,' he said with a grin. 'Anyway, there's too much in our past to give up now.'

'What exactly?' I knew of the Zionist Movement, but not how it had come about.

'Don't you know *why* we must have a homeland? Haven't you read about the Dreyfus case?'

I had not. Chaim impressed me because he was well-read and knowledgeable. I felt drawn to him. He began to explain as clearly as he could whilst we walked side by side.

'Dreyfus was a captain in the French army. He was Jewish and considered himself fully assimilated into French culture. But in 1880 he was accused of spying for the Germans and handing over vital information. He was put on trial in Paris with no real evidence against him except an obviously forged letter signed *D*. The main case for the prosecution was that Dreyfus was disloyal to France because he was a Jew.'

'That was ridiculous!' I exclaimed.

'Of course. We could never imagine it, but he was found guilty, stripped of his honour and sentenced to imprisonment on Devils Island.'

'Didn't anyone protest?' I asked.

'Yes. Many intelligent people wrote letters to newspapers and complained to the government that this was pure hatred and distrust of the Jews, for no good cause.'

'I don't understand it. I have never encountered anti-Semitism of any kind,' I said. 'All my life in the States I have moved in a secure circle where it is okay to be Jewish. No-one ever refused me entrance to a hotel or shouted obscenities at me.'

'Be thankful,' said Chaim seriously.

'I know that my father was picked out and ridiculed in the Russian army simply for his religious beliefs,' I added.

'Then you are aware that pogroms took place in Eastern Europe and that persecutions are still going on today. You are lucky nothing has ever touched you.'

'Go on,' I said, pulling an orange from the tree to share with Chaim. As I carefully broke it into segments I realised how little I knew. I handed him half. With his mouth full of sweet juice, Chaim continued the story.

'A young reporter from an Austrian newspaper was sent to cover the trial. He knew there was a miscarriage of justice simply to appease the public. When the trial was all over, with Dreyfus in chains, our man stood in the streets of Paris and heard good, civilised Frenchmen shouting, *'Down with the Jews. Death to the Jews!'*

'So one man taints all,' I said.

'Exactly. Even if he is innocent. As a Jew, Dreyfus had no defence against racism and bigots.' Chaim ate his segments thoughtfully. 'None of us have.'

'What happened in the end?' I was thoroughly intrigued.

'The real villain was eventually uncovered. Dreyfus was declared innocent and reinstated in the army, although the years of suffering had left him a broken man. But the news reporter found it a revelation. He realised that the only defence for Jews was to have a State of their own. A land where sovereignty would protect them from the anti-Semitic accusations of the civilised world.'

'That was some perceptive journalist,' I said.

'Right,' said Chaim. 'His name was Theodore Herzl. Ever heard of him?'

'We live in Herzlia!' I exclaimed.

'His vision brought your family here,' said Chaim. 'By the 1890s he had convened the first Zionist Congress in Basle, inviting leaders of world Jewry to attend. His message was that the Jews had to return to Zion.'

'I know the rest,' I said. 'Papa has been a Zionist all his life. We kids collected dollars for the Jewish National Fund. Papa used to purchase parcels of land over here. Barmitzvah boys thought he was mad giving them gifts of land in Palestine on bits of paper so that one day they could settle here. I've known his ideals all my life. I never knew the event that gave birth to them.'

'There are many more events, Harriett.' Chaim put his arm around me. 'Persecutions that go as far back as Masada.' He turned me around to face him and looked serious. 'You really ought to know just why you are here.'

'Chaim, why are you here?'

'I came fired with a feeling of impending disaster at what is happening in Germany. We must have a land of our own once more. And as quickly as possible.' He kissed the tip of my nose and laughed. 'You look so serious, Harriett. Don't be sad, be proud. You are living in historic times. Just be aware of that.'

I knew now that I was, but I did not mention it to anyone else.

The topping out of our house in Herzlia took place at the end of August. All the family were photographed cheerfully waving to the world from the flat roof. J.L. and Sol had most reason to feel proud, since they had helped with every process of the construction. Later, we stood together on the hill in front of our house admiring the breathtaking view of the sea.

'Do you see all that sand right to the sea shore?' said J.L. pointing to the coastline. 'Well, one day that will all be covered with beautiful villas and hotels.'

Sol, Esther and I looked at one another and mouthed 'He's mad!' We did not have his vision.

Soon afterwards we left Mrs. Mandelbaum's rooms for our new home. Here we celebrated the Jewish New Year together, emotionally and happily. My father's dream was coming true.

My parents became novice farmers. Sol was training to be a real farmer at an agricultural school nearby. In his spare time he helped alongside father, who started a small-holding on his surrounding land that spread towards the neighbouring Arab village of Jalil. They tilled land that had lain fallow for centuries. Cows, chickens, goats and a horse were brought in. J.L. was determined to become self-sufficient, often exchanging pleasantries and farming ideas with his Arab neighbours. At long last he was farming in the Holy Land.

The container bringing our furniture and possessions from the States had arrived. Now we were able to put everything in its place. Our cherry wood beds stood elegantly in the whitewashed bedroom as Esther and I unpacked our belongings. Outside, father and Sol were unloading the last of the furniture when a young couple stopped to talk to them. I watched as they walked around inspecting the huge container.

'It's large enough to live in,' they said. 'It would do for us. Can we have it?'

J.L. threw back his head and roared with laughter. Then he opened his arms to the sky.

'Visionaries!' he declared. 'Come into the house. I'll arrange it.'

He had the large container deposited a little way off where this immigrant family turned it into a very comfortable, habitable dwelling-place. Several containers ended up this way because there were many destitute, illegal immigrants searching for a foothold in Zion. They could not afford the expensive certificate from the British Mandate quota, but had managed to enter Palestine with the help of the Jewish Agency, often escaping from countries where they had left hurriedly to avoid persecution. They were resilient and practical people who took advantage of whatever was on offer. Anything to build themselves a secure future.

Life in the little hamlet of Azor Gimel, Herzlia, was reminiscent of our beach holidays in Woodmont, Connecticut. There was the same sense of freedom and anticipation that the future was good. The climate was more treacherous, as I had found out, but I kept myself covered in

the sun and wore a sun hat. I did not suffer any more serious
sun-burn. Our crowd of friends, girls and boys, often gathered
together in the evenings to discuss serious matters.

'We're having a Sheep Roast on the beach tonight,' said
Chaim one afternoon, introducing me to some young men he
had brought over from the main town. 'I know it's short
notice, but Sol is with us. Just make sure you come. We need
you as a decoy.'

'What do you want me to do?' I asked.

'Keep the British happy and out of our way.' He laughed
at my expression. 'Do you think you can do that, Harriett?'

After my experiences with naval officers on the SS
Vulcania I knew that I could.

'Just do as you are told,' advised Sol.

The heat of the day spread into a warm evening. As the
beach darkened and the sun set against the horizon, the sea
lay calm and vast under a moonless sky. Out and away in the
distance a light flickered and died, then repeated the signal.

Everyone set to fixing the fire, staking the barbecue,
joking and noisily singing songs, generally making merry
around the camp site. When two British coastguards on
horseback cantered up to investigate, we greeted them
happily, generously offering to share our meal with them. It
was a relaxed and amicable gathering.

Sol quietly gave me my orders. 'Make friends with them.
Ask them to give you a ride along the beach.'

He pointed to the stretch of sand disappearing away in the
distance. I nodded, but felt very apprehensive.

'I love horses,' I said to the guards, offering them another
piece of bread and meat which they were happily devouring.

'What's your name, luv?'

'I'm Harriett. My friend here is Susan.' We gave them our
most alluring smiles.

'I'm Sergeant Cooper. You can call me Don. He's Bill.'

Even in the twilight Bill seemed to blush.

Don't catch any poor fish with that line of yours! I knew that I would.

'I had a horse once, in the States. Her name was Nellie. I miss her.' I looked very wistful, stroking the haunches of his mount.

'Like to try mine?' said Don.

'Can Susan come too?'

The two men eagerly lifted Susan and me on to each of their horses. We wobbled and screamed as the animals moved. I dug in my heels rather too hard so that my mount cantered with Don running after me, until I reined in and let him jump up in the saddle behind me. Susan was playing a similar game.

'Sorry, I'm out of practice,' I gasped. 'Hold me tight and gallop along the sands.'

Neither soldier needed much persuading. With arms around their pretty cargo, they raced against each other, way along the darkened beach between the Arab villages of Jalil and Sidni Ali, farther and farther from the barbecue party, the noise fading into the distance. Half an hour later we came to a breathless halt and dismounted laughingly on to the sands.

'Give us a kiss!' said Don.

'A small one, when we get back,' I said, disentangling myself from his arms.

'God, you're damn pretty! What's an American lass doing in this hell hole?'

'I love it here,' I said. 'Sun, sea and sand. It's got everything!'

'Bleeding Arabs and Jews fighting over it, with we British in the middle.' He frowned, suddenly thoughtful. 'Fair haired, blue eyed gal like you, you're not a Jew are you?'

'Aren't I?'

His face hardened as realisation struck home.

'Oh Lord, something's up, Bill. We must get back immediately. I think they are up to something!'

Susan and I were hoisted unceremoniously on to their mounts and galloped back along the beach. The fire of the barbecue was dimming down, the group sat with arms around each other, humming folk songs. Several couples looked as though they had fallen asleep in each others arms. Everything was serene.

Sol came forward to berate us.

'Where the hell have you been?' he yelled at me. 'You wait till our father hears what you've been up to.'

Don interceded. 'They did not come to any harm,' he said sheepishly, feeling he had made a mistake about us.

Sol calmed down. Chaim walked over and shook their hands.

'Thank you for looking after them,' he said. 'They are very naughty girls.' The way he smacked my bottom was more like a congratulatory caress.

Fear and excitement merged into relief as the coastguards saluted, made their farewells and trotted away. The luck of the game had stayed with us that night.

Minutes later several 'courting' and 'sleeping' couples sat up, quickly rose to their feet and gathered together their few possessions. They silently followed Chaim and his group into the orange groves. Here younger parents and others of our village, hidden in prearranged places, were ready to collect the illegal immigrants and disperse them to homes where welcoming families could shelter them from the British. The Jewish Agency would then help to set them up in their new homeland.

Chapter 8
Tel Aviv (1935 – 1936)

By September it was arranged that Esther go to Tel Aviv daily to complete her schooling at Sofra. She travelled back and forth on the Egged bus, over an hour's journey each way from Herzlia to Tel Aviv. She never complained. In the evenings we would sit under the pomegranate tree in our garden, sucking the sweet juice of the fruit and spitting out pips, reading or talking. I admitted I would go back to the States eventually, but oddly enough living in Herzlia gave me no feeling of being out of place. So long as my parents were around I always felt I had a settled base, that I was 'at home' and part of the fabric of the country. However, I was no longer a schoolgirl like Esther. I needed something of my own to do.

We were in continuous touch by letter with our family in the States. Anyone who knew us passed on messages or introductions to new immigrants with our address. So it happened that one day we were visited by the Brown sisters, Evie and Helen, both slim, good-looking girls in their early twenties. I got along fine with them, discussing the wonders of the cruise which we had all appreciated, before they started outlining their future plans.

'We've teamed up with two other girls, Bernice and Doris, on our voyage over,' said Helen.

'I was secretary back home. It should not be difficult to find work here. We're all going to set up in Tel Aviv and take jobs,' said Evie.

This seemed eminently sensible to me.

'I'm going to do the same,' I announced. 'I am going to learn shorthand and typing and get a job as well.'

'You're an enterprising girl,' said Chaim that evening when I recounted my plans to him.

'I'm just marking time until the year has passed, then I'll take my trip home,' I promised.

I arranged to attend a school in Allenby Street, Tel Aviv, to learn to type. For a time I caught the early bus with Esther to take up my lessons. The classroom was bare except for chairs at tables with typewriters. Everyone had to type in unison until we got the hang of it. *The quick black fox jumped over the lazy dog..* It surprised me how easy that was and I quickly reached sixty words a minute.

Shorthand was less simple. I paid to have individual shorthand lessons from a girl called Sarah, whom I met on the ship coming over. She had learned Millers' shorthand in New York. This was not the Pitman's shorthand that everyone else used. I struggled with the slashes and wiggles until eventually I could read back my own shorthand, although nobody else could. I would never have passed an examination with it.

Over coffee and a chat one afternoon with the Brown girls, Evie and Helen offered me the independence I had been waiting for.

'We have found a small, very elite hotel,' said Evie. 'The Atlantic Hotel run by a lovely couple.'

'There's a room on the roof which we are renting,' said Helen.

'No bathroom, no kitchen,' said Doris. 'But there is a lift to the top.'

'It's furnished with a table, chairs, a cupboard and beds. Would you like to share with us?'

Would I!

'It's £4 a month - £1 a month each. Bernice has found another place so we can offer you hers.'

When I told my parents they were very easy about it. They knew the Brown girls. Also I had family in Tel Aviv, so it was fine by them. My parents supported me without any fuss.

I arrived in the roof-room next day with my holdall to find that there were only two beds up there.

'We sleep two to a bed,' grinned Helen.

Somehow we managed it. We were young, we were independent and it was our own space. Nobody bothered us up there. We often sat talking long into the night, sharing a cigarette amongst the four of us. There was nowhere to cook, so we ate out in restaurants because food was cheap. We were thrilled if someone invited us to dine with them and we did not have to pay.

To me it was still important to be with my family every weekend. On Friday afternoons I took the bus home to Herzlia.

'How are you managing?' Mama asked over Shabbat dinner.

'Just fine,' I said airily. 'We have everything we need in our room. Helen brought the cutlery. I took a milk jug. Doris found a sugar basin. We haven't bought a thing.' I refrained from mentioning cigarettes.

'Where did you get it all from?' J.L. suddenly looked serious.

'When we eat out we take something we need,' I said proudly.

'So you are all thieves?' He was not at all pleased.

'No, we are not!'

'Yes, you are. People make a living out of their restaurant. When you take things, they have to replace them. That costs them money. That's stealing.'

I felt rather shamefaced. I had not thought of it like that and I never did it again.

Chaim and I met to talk that evening. I was full of my independent life in Tel Aviv. He seemed pensive.

'You seem much more mature,' he said. 'Are you still going back to America next year?'

'Oh yes!' I said, and meant it.

In Tel Aviv someone told me about a job that might suit me. It was for a man working alone in one room who needed a typist. So long as I did not have to do shorthand I felt confident enough to apply. I duly presented myself for an interview.

'Can you type accurately?' He was Jewish, very tall, cultured and good-looking. He spoke English fluently.

'Sure, I can type nearly seventy words a minute,' I said, confidently entering the world of work at the age of seventeen on £4 a month.

My first job was to write sixty letters to British Members of Parliament in an attempt to get Palestine accepted into the Commonwealth. It seemed an eminently suitable solution to the problem of self-government. I set about the task with great enthusiasm. Unfortunately, in trying to type sixty letters without errors I used up three hundred sheets of letter headings. My boss was not pleased when he found I had worked through all his headed stationery.

The summer was the hottest I could remember. I managed to swim most days, either in the early morning or else after work when the heat of the day had subsided. I joined dozens of other young women and men splashing around in the warm water or playing beach ball on the shore, making new friends when they threw the ball my way or offered me a cigarette.

One girl in particular, Malka, with deep brown eyes and long silky hair, met up with me regularly and we soon became confidants.

'Apart from boring work in the office, this is like a continual holiday for me,' I said, surprised at myself for admitting I was having such a good time.

'Well, I am still at college during term,' said Malka, laying back on her towel and fanning out her long black hair to dry. 'But I try to go sight-seeing as much as possible.'

'I haven't been anywhere,' I said, covering myself from the sun with my towel. 'Except for the voyage from the States I've hardly seen anything of this country.'

'Come with me to Haifa next weekend. Can you?'

'It was the first place we landed,' I remembered.

'My aunt and uncle have a villa on Mount Carmel. It is very smart. Please will you come? I would love someone of my age to keep me company. They are dear people but they are ancient - in their forties!'

I laughed. 'My parents are extremely old at that rate.' Strangely, I had never thought of them as elderly.

It was arranged that instead of going to Herzlia, I would stay with Malka at her relatives' villa for a couple of days. On Friday afternoon we took the train to Haifa, then hired a taxi to the smart district on the side of Mount Carmel overlooking the shimmering bay. The white-washed villa stood above an arbour of cypress trees which shaded the steps to their front door.

'They will make you very welcome,' Malka assured me as the maid opened the door. The only problem was that they had forgotten Malka was coming, and although they were very hospitable they could not avoid a previous engagement on Saturday night.

'It will mean that you two girls are all alone for the evening,' worried Malka's aunt.

'We will be all right,' said Malka. 'I'll show Harriett the night life in town.'

'That you won't,' exclaimed her uncle. 'Two beautiful young girls like you must be chaperoned.' He turned to his wife.

'Perhaps our neighbours, Maurice and Albert, will consider entertaining them while we are out,' he said. 'You would like them. They are very distinguished and erudite.'

I was not sure if *erudite* sounded entertaining, but I had to defer since I was the visitor.

Maurice and Albert (pronounced the French way) turned out to be two elderly brothers, well over forty, who were more than happy to entertain eighteen year old girls for dinner.

'They have brought elegant living to a fine art,' I whispered to Malka, as we sat at their dining table laden with cut glass and silver cutlery. The first course of baked goat cheese was new to me.

'This is delicious,' I said appreciatively. I knew good food when I tasted it, and the rest of the meal was equally excellent.

'Well, we are French, so we know about good cooking,' said Maurice.

'And about wonderful wines,' echoed Albert.

He uncorked another bottle, since they had served different wines to complement every course. Recalling J.L.'s warning not to get tiddly, I only tasted a sip from each glass, but the wine was potent enough to make my toes curl and blur my vision. I can imagine how amused the brothers were at our youthful ignorance, but they seemed polite enough to allow us to gabble on about our ideas and views of the times.

'I have promised myself that I will return to the States next year,' I said, feeling relaxed enough to confide in these strangers.

'Don't you like it here?' asked Malka, surprised. 'You said it was like a holiday!'

'Sure. But I am an American. I want to go back and start a career for myself.'

'As what?' asked Albert.

Here I faltered. I really had no idea.

'Something grown-up I expect,' interjected Maurice, rising from the table. 'Now let us retire to the Fumiere, our smoking room.'

This was a small intimate room with comfortable chairs and large cushions scattered on the floor near an open window. Outside, the sounds of the night crickets chirped in the blackness. Albert lay back against a cushion, lit a cigarette and handed it to Malka. The sweet smell of smoke pervaded the air.

'I don't smoke,' she said, sitting on the floor.

'Do you smoke?' Albert enquired, handing it to me.

'Of course,' I said, putting the proffered cigarette to my lips and drawing on it. Unfamiliar sickly smoke filled my mouth.

'Yuk! This is disgusting!' I exclaimed, pulling it away from my mouth. 'It's so sweet.'

Albert laughed at me. 'It's hashish. You'll get used to it.'

Suddenly my vision cleared.

'No thanks. I'd rather light one of my own,' I said, rummaging in my bag to produce a crumpled packet of Players that had lain hidden there for a week.

Maurice and Albert were visibly disappointed that neither Malka nor I was under the influence of either alcohol or cannabis, but they remained gentlemen and led us back to our villa before aunt and uncle returned from their party to find us safely asleep in bed.

The season of Chanukah approached before I knew it. Early in December, I left work and walked along Rehov Herzl to Rehov Ahad Ha'am towards the Herzlia Gymnasium. Crowds of people milled around, cheerful and expectant. Everyone was singing *Maotzur* and the *Hatikvah*, waiting for the first candle of the huge street Chanukiah to be lit on the first night of the festival.

When the moment came, a runner held high a burning torch to light the first candle. The flame blazed to the cheers of the crowd. Then he handed the torch to another runner and accompanied by joyful youngsters they started their relay run from Tel Aviv along the dangerous twisting road to Jerusalem. There, where the age-old dream of our capital city held firm, they would give light to the Chanukiah in the Old City. That small flame of freedom, which Mama and Papa had lit in our home every year of my life, was here huge and visible. A light of hope and freedom. At that moment I knew these were my people, this was my country, this was *my* dream. I picked up my father's vision of the future for the Jewish people with an overwhelming sense of gratitude to my parents for instilling in me the pride of being Jewish.

That weekend I returned home eagerly to tell my parents how I felt. Afterwards, I went out to find Chaim to let him know I had caught the flame as he had. I walked around looking for him but he was not there. Eventually I asked Mrs. Mandelbaum. She shook her head sadly.

'His father sent for him urgently,' she said. 'He has had to return to the States.'

CHAPTER 9

Seligman & Levitsky (1936)

When Purim arrived in the springtime, I had forgotten all about Chaim. This was a joyful festival celebrating the biblical story of Queen Esther and her success in saving her people from evil anti-Semites. We knew these murderers were an ever present threat in Nazi Germany, but to prove our stoicism Tel Aviv was decked with flags. There were floats in the street and people donned fancy dress, dancing through the night to celebrate the ancient reprieve. We girls were inundated with invitations.

'We're partying every night this week!' Helen and Evie exclaimed happily.

'So am I,' I countered. By this time our circles of friends were diverging and we were often invited to different affairs.

'Mrs. Prochevesky is holding her annual Odef Meretz Purim Ball at the San Remo hotel,' said Evie. 'She organises everything, but you have to pay for your own food and drinks. Have you been invited ?'

'Sure,' I said. 'I hope I can keep up my energy!'

Everybody who was anybody converged on the San Remo for the last night of Purim. Malka and I met outside and went in together. The ballroom was decked with streamers and balloons. The orchestra, in full evening dress, struck up the latest quickstep *Anything Goes*. We were caught up in the excitement and revelry of it all. What a country where Jewish festivals were national holidays!

I sat shyly at a table alongside Malka until a young man approached to dance the quick-step with me.

'Excuse me,' interrupted another, so that I was whisked away across the ballroom for the next dance and the one after that.

'You certainly like dancing,' said one tall, dark, attractive partner.

His statement sounded like interrogation.

'I do! It's good exercise and great fun,' I countered. 'I like it more than anything. What's wrong with that?'

'Nothing at all.' He swung me out onto the floor, gliding and swaying to the music as the band played *Won't You Change Partners and Dance With Me?*

'I'm a lawyer,' he said, introducing himself while dancing. 'Call me Mac.'

'I'm Harriett, a secretary,' I said.

'The perfect fit then,' he grinned.

He danced divinely, guiding me around the dance floor. *Heaven, I'm in Heaven* went the next song. My eyes were half-shut, my head against his shoulder as the song ended. I wanted to stay with him all night.

'Look, I have to dance with someone else,' said Mac, suddenly steering me back to my table, leaving me to fan my reddened face with my handkerchief. Was I blushing with embarrassment? On the dance floor I could see Malka, Evie and Helen twirling around with partners, whilst I sat alone feeling deflated and left out.

'You look hot and bothered,' said a young man with a round, jolly face who came to sit beside me.

'I can't dance another step,' I panted loudly, putting out my hand to shake his. 'I'm Harriett.'

'Oh, I know who you are,' he interrupted. 'I'm Gabriel. Gaby for short. May I get you a drink?'

'That's very kind of you. No alcohol though.'

Gaby was short, tubby and full of good-humour. I recovered my composure as we sipped drinks and exchanged views.

'I'm having a wonderful time dancing with so many people I've never met before!' I confided.

'Good. I helped to organise this function. Especially the charity tombola. How do you feel about helping out tonight, selling some raffle tickets?'

'I should be delighted,' I said.

This would be a wonderful opportunity to meet up again with Mac, the tall, good-looker who had taken me in his arms earlier. I happily selected a set of raffle books and made my way across the floor. Mac seemed to be engrossed with a group of people, so I ignored him and worked my way around the ballroom selling dozens of tickets before reporting back to Gaby.

'You certainly have a knack of parting people from their money! In future, I am co-opting you to help on my charity committee,' he said cheerfully.

'Any time,' I said, as the orchestra struck up a tango.

All at once Mac was by my side guiding me onto the floor, his hand on my waist, moving me in time to the music.

'You are quite a dancer,' he said.

'So are you! I could dance with you all night,' I ventured.

'My dear, sweet, darling girl,' Mac said. 'You cheer me up and I love you for it!'

No one had ever said they loved me before. I glowed with pleasure.

By the end of the evening I had made two new friends. Gaby, who persuaded me to join his social committee to help raise money for a children's playground, and Mac, who promised to take me out dancing again.

As is often the case, the way up is not what you know, but whom you know. On one of my visits to Sarah for yet another shorthand lesson, her sister, Ida, remarked to me, 'I work for the lawyers Seligman & Levitsky. I could do with a girl in the office as receptionist, answer the phone, do the filing. Would you help? You would earn £5 a month.'

I jumped at the offer since my first boss had not received one positive reply to his letters. Many Members of Parliament had not replied at all. He was relieved to let me go.

I arrived early at Seligman & Levitsky's office, confident and ready to take up my post at the reception desk. A little later an impeccably dressed gentleman entered the office, took a double look at me and enquired in a soft English accent, 'Who are you?'

'Harriett Gold. I'm the receptionist here. May I ask your name?'

'Max Seligman. I am your boss,' he said with a twinkle in his eye. 'I hope you will like it here.'

I did enjoy working in the busy law office headed by Max Seligman. Later on I learned he had been born in Wales. He had come to Palestine as an ardent Zionist when he was nineteen. At the time I met him he was in his early thirties, a happy family man with two young daughters.

By then, we room-mates had left our roof hideaway and moved to a purpose-built hostel with individual bedrooms. There was a kitchen for sharing and a bathroom with a coin meter for hot water. We were always short of money and still shared one bath for two people.

'You go in first this time – I'll go in first next time,' we agreed with each other.

When I sank into steaming water knowing that I could pay for my own bath without having to share it with anyone else, I felt at last I was in the lap of luxury.

My vivacious friend, Phyllis, whom I had met on my arrival in Palestine was newly married to Yadim, the son of a judge. Hers was the first smart wedding I had ever been invited to. The reception was at the King David Hotel in Jerusalem and everybody who was anybody had been invited, including me! Now that she was settled in a home of her own, she happily invited me around for lunch and a good gossip once or twice a week. This was my main meal of the day, for which I was very grateful. We never veered from being the best of friends.

One of the young lawyers in the firm, Arnold, had also taken a shine to me. He and his wife, Queenie, were in the centre of the social whirl of young, highly educated Jewish intellectuals.

'Harriett, come to our house tonight. We're having a party,' Arnold said one afternoon and promptly took me home with him. To my astonishment, the first person I was introduced to was Mac. I blushed.

'We already know each other,' he said.

It was an evening that introduced me to dear people who liked me for myself. Up to that time all my friends had been mostly Americans, but Arnold's friends made me feel completely welcome, drawing me into another world with another viewpoint. This crowd were mainly Sabras, Jews born in Palestine. In my ignorance I had thought all foreign people were, well foreign! But they were not at all. They were as cultured, often much more cultured and sophisticated than anyone I had imagined in my wildest dreams. They were all far more highly educated than I was. Without realising it, I was mixing with the young elite of the country who came from comfortably settled families of five or six generations, owning large factories or pardessim, which were orange groves. Most had been sent to Europe to be educated, but all had come back to settle. Everyone spoke a minimum of three languages; perfect Hebrew of course, English and at least one other European language. I felt a real ignoramus. I did not even speak Hebrew.

I had already joined the English Speaking Forum with the Brown girls and other American friends. We were active members, often taking part in debates. I enjoyed the intellectual aspect, maybe more than a few other members. However, I began to realise I should make the effort to speak Hebrew with my Hebrew friends.

Eventually, at one party where everyone spoke English simply because I was there, I declared aloud, 'Right, if you don't all speak Hebrew to me, I'm going home!'

There was an astonished silence. Then conversation continued in a language I found hard to comprehend. It was a very big struggle for me, but they admired my stand. It took many weeks of hilarious coaching but I was determined. I finally made it and learned to speak Hebrew. At last, I hoped, I was one foreign girl who was completely accepted into the local society.

*

Max Seligman's firm dealt with all types of law, from conveyancing and probate to advocacy. Initially, I was just given copy typing. Having to type eight copies of eight pages of a conveyancing document, read it through with another typist for mistakes and then re-type it because of errors, bored the hell out of me. It showed. Soon I was asked to take over in other areas. That way I learnt the intricacies of managing an office.

One morning Ida came in to announce that she was getting married.

'So I'm out of here,' she said gaily. 'You can take on my job as office manager if you want.'

That was my great good fortune. The role of office organiser was going to suit me fine, but I had to organise something else first.

I knocked boldly on Mr. Seligman's door and entered. He looked at me over a pile of papers and through a haze of cigarette smoke.

'What can I do for you, Harriett?'

I took a deep breath.

'Mr. Seligman, I think I should get a raise of ten shillings a month.' I paused, took another breath and continued. 'Because I'm now doing a lot more than I was hired to do.'

He tapped the cigarette ash into an ashtray and smiled to himself.

'Well, I'll give it to you, but I've got a condition.'

I was really taken aback. I mean just what kind of condition would a raise in salary require?

I whispered nervously, 'What's the condition?'

He grinned at me and pointed to my feet.

'That you stop wearing ankle socks and start wearing stockings.'

'Oh, yes, I'll agree to that!'

I knew that stockings were expensive items, but did Mr. Seligman?

'I would need a raise of a pound,' I added tentatively.

I must have looked dazed with delight when I walked back to my desk. I was going to earn six pounds a month.

*

To the surprise of my Tel Aviv friends I always returned to Azor Gimmel at the weekends. My parents never said, 'You must come'. If they had, I probably should have stayed in town. However, over time I realised that farming was not as successful as J.L. had hoped and that finances were tight. One weekend Mama looked especially strained and tired.

'Come to Tel Aviv next week,' I said to cheer her up. 'I'll take you on a little shopping spree, like in the old days.'

'Harriett, I will come in two weeks time. My cousin's daughter, Mildred, is arriving then to stay in Palestine and I would like to meet her when she arrives.'

'Another relative!' I exclaimed.

My mother paused. 'She is not well. Her family think it will do her good to visit the Holy Land. They want to know if she can share with you.'

I pulled a face. 'I hardly live in luxury. Besides, I only have a single bed.'

'Could you look for a nicer place?' Mother pleaded. This seemed to be important to her. 'Mildred will contribute to the expenses.'

'If I have to,' I said, without much enthusiasm.

The following week I found a large furnished room with two beds in an apartment in Shenkin Street, on the corner of Rothschild Boulevard. I moved in two days later promising to keep in touch with Helen and Evie Brown.

As soon as she arrived, Mildred and I immediately hit it off.

'You're a Meltzer!' I exclaimed when I saw her fair hair and blue eyes. 'You look more like my sister than Esther!'

I told her of the constant teasing I had received from my uncles when I was young. Mildred laughed and embraced me. We found instant rapport with each other.

'Tonight, I'm going to introduce you to *everyone*,' I said.

'Not tonight.' Mildred sank onto her bed. 'I need to get over my travelling - but you go.'

'Well, I will introduce you to Mac at least, when he calls for me.'

Over the next weeks I determined to show Mildred everything and introduce her to new friends.

'I enjoy your company, Harriett. I love being in Palestine. I feel so much better here,' she confided.

She took a job in a nearby office. We spent our leisure time together talking about everything and every individual in the crowd of friends we now shared. But it became increasingly evident that Mildred's energy level was not the same as mine. She would make excuses to go to bed early. Occasionally she stayed in bed all day. She did not keep her job.

'You really are a lazy-bones,' I admonished her.

One weekend in Herzlia, while Mildred was dozing outside under the pomegranate tree and I was helping Mama with the washing up, I mentioned Mildred's laziness. Mama dried her hands on her apron and turned to face me.

'Mildred is dying,' she said quietly.

I was so shocked I could hardly speak for inner tears. I had had no idea. How cruel fate was to the innocent and beautiful.

After that, I never mentioned it to Mildred, but tried to make her time as enjoyable as possible. We went to the pictures together, out to dine; visited relations. I introduced her to Mac, in whom I confided and who was kindness itself. Eventually, it became clear that she would have to return to the States.

'Thank you, Harriett darling, for the wonderful time we have spent together,' said Mildred, hugging me for the last time. 'You will write to me about everyone and everything? You promise?'

I promised. 'I love writing letters, Mildred dear. You can be sure I will write to you *forever.*'

Mac and I helped put her luggage on to the bus to Haifa. When it drove away and she was out of sight, I burst into tears and cried on Mac's shoulder for a long time.

Mac and I were now seeing a lot of each other. I met his mother, father and married sister, we all got along fine. He never mentioned marriage, but he sure loved my company.

Mac is taking me to the *Tuberculosis Charity Ball* next Sunday night,' I told Esther at the weekend.

It was one of the main social events of the year. I carefully packed my best evening gown of blue moiré trimmed with gold, which I had had made for Phyllis' wedding. I knew I would look stunning in it. I was exhilarated at the thought of dancing with Mac, like Ginger Rogers and Fred Astaire, and melting into his arms. Maybe this night he would get romantic and propose. I was not sure of my answer but it would be nice to be asked!

That weekend I stayed in Tel Aviv washing my hair, doing my nails, so that I would look perfect for the ball. On Sunday afternoon, just as I was about to get dressed, I had a visitor. It was Mac.

'Harriett. I'm not going tonight.' Mac had called round to give me this piece of 'good' news.

'But I am looking forward to it!' I exclaimed.

He looked embarrassed. 'The exams come up soon. My mother says I've spent too much time neglecting my studies. She feels I should put more effort into it, rather than go dancing.' He trailed off.

'Sure!' I exploded. 'If your mother says don't go!'

I shrugged him away.

When he left, I was mad. Furious at him for being such a wimp. Scornful of myself for ever wanting to go out with him. Desolate that I was not going to the ball after all. I lay on the bed sobbing loudly, banging my fist into the pillow.

On Monday morning, the office telephone was constantly busy with my friends asking if I was okay and where had I been last night?

'I had a real bad headache,' I said truthfully.

'Meet up with us tomorrow,' said Evie. 'We are having a night out.'

'Okay,' I said. I was not going to let any man get me down. I looked my best when I met up with my girl friends in the cafe.

'Hello! You're Harriett, aren't you?' A debonair man approached me. He spoke with a thick accent. 'May I introduce myself. I am Yona.'

'Do I know you?' He seemed familiar.

'I am a good friend of Arnold. We have met at parties.'

I had been so involved with Mac that I had never noticed him before, but I was perfectly happy to speak to him now.

'I should like to get to know you better. Would you care to have dinner with me tomorrow night?' He was a fast worker. I knew he was not my type, but what the hell.

'Sure,' I said, suddenly remembering that he had been pointed out to me as a *divorced man!* I could take care of myself!

So by Wednesday, I was back in the swing again.

CHAPTER 10

Palestine (1936–1937)

The Chamsin, an uncomfortably warm wind from the desert, sent temperatures soaring as it did every year. One evening when the intense heat of the day lingered on in a warm haze, I was invited by friends, Suzy and Joe, to a dinner party. Yona was also a guest and conversation over the meal started lightly enough. Which books had been read? I mentioned that I had just finished *The Stars Look Down* by Dr. Cronin and was starting to read *The Arab Woman and the Palestine Problem* by Mrs. Mogannam. I was an avid reader, books were always important to me.

Everyone agreed that the latest films, *The Great Ziegfeld* and *Clive of India*, were undoubtedly the best to see.

Afterwards the talk moved towards more serious matters which aroused my awareness of impending events.

'There are ominous laws being passed in Germany. Anti-Jewish laws,' said Joe, offering cigarettes to his guests after dinner. 'Immigration to Palestine needs to be stepped up. We have to get our people out of there, British quotas or not.'

I took a cigarette while Yona held his lighter for me. I inhaled delicately and smiled at him. Then he turned back to Joe.

'I hear the Grand Mufti in Jerusalem wants to stop Jewish immigration altogether,' he said.

'Even though we pay astronomical prices to buy land in Palestine?' said Suzy.

'He's called for a General Strike. No Arab to work until transfer of land to Jews is ended.'

'If the Arab bus drivers stop work then Jewish bus drivers will take over,' said Yona. 'If they want to leave their produce un-harvested then Jewish farmers will have to work longer hours. But we must also arm ourselves against increasing Arab attacks on our settlements.'

'You can understand their fears. They see themselves becoming a minority. Economically and politically,' said Suzy 'We know how that feels.'

'Maybe,' replied Joe. 'But here in Palestine both Arabs and Jews are under the yoke of the British.' That remark brought general assent as the conversation veered back to lighter matters.

Next Friday afternoon when I went to catch the two o'clock bus home to Herzlia, I had to cadge a lift because there was a strike and none was running. Surprisingly, Sol was not at home that weekend either. Even more unusual was the sound of gunfire in the distance. There were marks on our front wall, which J.L. pointed out to me as being evidence of bullets. The unrest was real enough.

Arab riots in Jaffa were quashed by the British. Curfews on both Jews and Arabs made the atmosphere uneasy. My parents did not seem too alarmed but I questioned J.L. anxiously about their safety. He assured me all was well.

'My friend and neighbour, the Mukhtar of Jalil, frequently takes tea in my house. He is as friendly as ever. Don't you worry. Arab and Jew get along fine together when we are left alone. We are both sons of Abraham.' My father smiled at me over his lemon tea. 'However, he has expressed an interest in something of mine,' he continued with his usual twinkle.

'Really?' I was not too interested. 'What?'

'You! He wants to buy you for his wife.'

I roared with laughter. 'What did you tell him?'

'I told him 'Okay.' He offered thirty five cows for you.'

'Papa!' I was indignant.

'The problem is - I don't want Arab cows. They are a different stock to mine. Unfortunately, he doesn't have any other cows. We bargained. I offered him Esther, but he only wants the blonde one with the blue eyes. So no deal!'

These two men had enjoyed haggling over me.

'It would help cement relations between Arab and Jew,' I retaliated. 'But I ain't going to be the one to do it!'

I secretly felt quite flattered. After all, it was the first proposal of marriage I ever had.

*

Although things appeared to have quietened down generally in Palestine, two criminal incidents had taken place. An engineer from Ramat Gan was stabbed many times and killed. Houses of certain people were found to have microphones embedded in the walls. Intricate radios and listening devices were discovered. Had the murdered man been a member of the Haganah? Or a spy for the British, or even the Germans? Who had killed him? The mystery was unsolved.

Then another Jew, a Dr. Baruch, was accused by an Arab of murdering his brother. For proof, bloodstained and torn clothing was found hidden in the doctor's house. There was a great hullabaloo. It was obviously a framed case. Now the Arab and six others had been arrested by the British.

Incidents on the curved, winding road to Jerusalem occurred more frequently. Always somebody, Arab or Jew, was being arrested or interrogated by the Palestine Police. The prison in the old fortress at Acre had been opened for use.

I faithfully reported all these happenings in my letters to Mildred. If I had any spare moment in the office, I would type out another page for her.

In December the gossip was all about HRH the Duke of Windsor. I thought he was 'pretty swell' and that there were high politics behind his abdication. I wrote to Mildred.

> 'All they want a king for is to give a good show of pomp and grandeur - but not one who wants to use his own brain when it comes to running the country. If this story about the Simpson dame is true and something comes of it - we certainly have to hand it to her. With all the beauties in the world and young ones - she a 39 year old woman gets the most eligible guy in the world. Well, American girls have what it takes, don't you know!'

Even though she was so far away, she was still my close confidant. When we were together I had confided in her of my dream.

'Cherish your dreams and they will come true,' she said.

My letters were pages long, filled with news and gossip. I wanted her to feel she was sharing in my life. I wanted to keep her alive.

*

At the office, my boss was becoming more involved in the political world. He had helped start a movement for changing Palestine into a Crown Colony. He was the President of the committee, Arnold was Treasurer and I was scribe. We had very many letters from people asking to join the movement. I was only in it to help out, not because I believed in it. The truth was that I did not understand enough to know whether or not I did believe in it. I reckoned Mr. Seligman would become very well known the world over because it was 'very big politics'. He was meeting Moshe Smilansky and Dr. Chaim Weizmann at the weekend.

Chanukah was again approaching. I kept myself happy ordering a new evening dress for the season of annual balls. It was exquisite, made in watermarked navy-blue satin. The waistline very high in front, emphasising my figure. The back was blouson, with a slit all the way down to open when I danced. It fitted my slender body wonderfully. I wore three gold flowers, pinned to the waist and golden shoes. When I appeared at the Chanukah ball, people went crazy about it.

'Is that a Paris model you're wearing?'

'Gee, Harriett, you certainly know how to dress the best!'

'Have you had a raise? It must have cost a small fortune!'

The dress had cost me $18 which was money well spent. I felt like the cat's whiskers and wrote Mildred all about it. I was happier about myself and more confident than ever before.

Life in Tel Aviv was vibrant and exciting. Our cultural experience was heightened by the arrival in Tel Aviv of Arturo Toscanini, the famous conductor, who had agreed to conduct the newly formed Palestine Orchestra. Our charity committee was part of the welcoming party for the great man. We gathered palm fronds, which we held high to make an arch under which Toscanini walked to his official reception. We were excited beyond measure to hear Mendelssohn played by our own orchestra in Tel Aviv. The atmosphere was electric when we rose as one for the Hatikvah.

At work, my secretarial services were often needed by visiting lawyers or clients who wished me to help out with their work. Some weeks I put in as much as ten extra hours. Although I never asked for payment, they were very generous. Here, at last, was the opportunity to start saving secretly for the dream I wanted to fulfil.

'I need some letters typed,' said Phil, an amiable, middle-aged Englishman on a business trip to Tel Aviv. He was watching me tap on my typewriter as he waited for his appointment. I smiled politely.

'Would you help me out? I could hire a typewriter. I could dictate them to you at my hotel,' he offered. 'I'll buy you dinner afterwards.'

It did not occur to me to refuse. He was such a nice man with an appealing accent and he made me laugh. During dinner I confided my dream to him of visiting London.

'You just let me know when you arrive, little lady, and I'll be there for you,' he said.

I sighed. 'It is only a dream!'

*

It was April 1937. My time in Palestine had flown by. The idea of my returning to America had long since lapsed. By now I could talk more freely about Mildred and of her cancer. I wrote regularly to her and in my last letter had recounted the present political situation:

'If you will think back you will remember that there were riots in Palestine not so very long ago. Also you will recollect that they were supposed to have stopped in October – officially. Well officially they did, but actually we have ever since had little incidents of sniping and that sort of stuff. The last few weeks it has all come to a head and there were outbreaks in Tiberias and last week in Jerusalem. The country was very tense. Bus service was stopped between Jaffa and Tel Aviv while other services had police escort. Again curfew was enforced in Jerusalem. It is now back to normal.. We hope it will stay quiet, but these things one can never tell. Outside of that

*'Little Arty' (Lieut.General Sir Arthur Wauchope, High
Commissioner) is now on leave in England and there are
rumours that he won't be coming back. There have been
other changes in Government departments – but none
that would particularly interest you. Except that 'Thank
the Lord,' the Chief Secretary has been replaced and we
all have hope that he will be less of an anti-Semite than
the last. Mind you I say 'less' and not 'not.''*

As always, I spent Friday night in Herzlia with my
parents, Sol and Esther. Mama lit the candles and J.L. made
kiddush as usual. During conversation over dinner he
suddenly turned to me.

'Harriett, it is nice to see you're settling down so
contentedly. You enjoy your work. You have good friends.
You seem to be having a wonderful time. I know we made a
pact years ago, but I hope you plan to stay. Will you?'

'Papa, you were right all along. I am happy to stay, but I
would like to see something of Europe as well. I thought I
might go in the summer.' My dream was out.

My mother exclaimed, 'Go to Europe on your own?' She
turned to my father. 'You hear? She says she's going alone!'

'I heard,' said J.L. 'She's going to Europe. What do you
want me to do?'

'But she's only nineteen years old!'

'So? If she lives in our house until she's forty, we can't
teach her more than we have taught her already,' reasoned my
father. 'Look, if she makes her bed she will lie in it. I won't lie
in her bed. She knows how to behave. There is no reason why
she should not go to Europe.'

I sat listening to their argument, waiting for a decision. If
they had said 'You're not going!' I am sure I would not have
gone. But J.L. actually believed there was no reason why I

should not go. It seemed I was going to get my wish. I wrote to Mildred in delight at the thought of my adventure.

Although I would never think of going out with Yona exclusively, he persisted in dating me two or three times a week.

'You are loads of fun to be with, but I can't take a man like you seriously,' I told him after he had wined and dined me.

He sat back, puffing a huge cigar. 'I don't take *any* woman seriously,' he said, raising his eyebrows. 'After all, a woman is a woman - but a cigar is a wonderful smoke!'

I burst out laughing. He was incorrigible!

One morning he turned up at the office while I was typing my letter to Mildred and placed a box tied with red ribbon on my desk.

'What is it?'

'It's something for your twentieth birthday.' He smiled. 'You know I am crazy about you. Open it.'

It was a dozen pairs of expensive silk stockings. I gasped.

'I can't accept this!' I exclaimed. 'It's too personal.'

'Well, after what you told me about your boss and the bobby socks, I thought you might need them to keep your job!' he teased. 'You can do what you like with them.'

'Thank you. I accept gratefully,' I said, having an idea.

Since the shop's label was on the box, I returned the gift next day and exchanged silk stockings for a deep blue dressing gown with orange lapels and a belt with an orange satin trim. It looked good on me. It would be perfect for staying in strange hotels.

CHAPTER 11

London (1937)

My father took care of everything. The six-week trip was arranged as my twentieth birthday present. Europe! I was to leave on the 2nd June from Haifa to Trieste; Trieste to Venice (two days); then Milan (one day); Lucerne (two days), on to Paris (five days). And finally to England for the rest of the time.

I busily wrote letters to relatives of my friends who lived abroad. All assured me they would put me up with pleasure, and would certainly be pleased to wine and dine me. On the threshold of my twenties, equipped with travellers cheques and armed with letters of introduction, I embarked alone on a journey to England. I was determined to have a swell time, especially since I had saved £60 of my own for spending.

At Haifa, on board the ship to Trieste, I chatted to another girl who seemed a little older and more sophisticated than I.

'I'm Debbie,' she said. 'I'm going to visit relatives in Paris. Our itineraries are the same until France. Shall we stick together?

'Sure, only I don't mind at all travelling alone. I love sailing,' I said.

How wrong I was. Almost the moment the ship left harbour I began to feel ill. It was not long before Debbie was ministering to me on my sea-sick bed.

'So much for travel!' I moaned.

By the time we docked at Trieste I was fully recovered. Together Debbie and I boarded the train to Venice; romantic city of canals and dreams. We registered at our hotel near the Grand Canal, then walked to the Rialto bridge to gaze at the gondoliers below. I was thrilled when they doffed their caps, shouting 'Bella!' to us.

'They mean you,' I said to Debbie, who was a sophisticated beauty.

'They mean us!' she insisted.

'It's a good place to come for a honeymoon,' I sighed.

By the time we reached Switzerland, Debbie and I had exchanged intimate stories and dreams. In the lounge of our Lausanne hotel, our animated conversation and laughter attracted several glances. A well-dressed gentleman walked over to us. He seemed very keen to engage in conversation. Where had we come from? Where were we going? He was pleasant company so we were perfectly happy to talk to him.

'May I invite you young ladies to join me for dinner?' he asked politely. Debbie and I glanced at each other, then exploded into giggles.

'All right,' we said, eventually calming down. After all, we were two independent gals and he was a gentleman. We saw no harm in it. We happily joined him at his table, but we were not so pleased when he ordered a la Carte without even consulting us.

'We'll have champagne.' He nodded to the waiter. Champagne on ice was promptly brought and the cork popped ceremoniously.

I was aghast at the array of expensive dishes that followed. I could hardly swallow since I was mentally totting up the price of the meal. It would cost at least half my savings even if I shared with Debbie. She seemed completely unconcerned and was happily tucking in.

My heart sank even further when the waiter courteously presented the bill. I apprehensively watched as it was checked expecting any minute to be asked for my contribution. I could have kicked myself when our companion smiled benignly at us, waved his hand to the waiter and said 'Charge it to my room'.

I wished I had enjoyed the dinner more!

*

'Next stop Paris,' shouted the stationmaster as the train pulled out of the station.

'Do you have somewhere to stay?' asked Debbie as we sat in the jolting carriage. 'I'm sure my relatives would accommodate you.'

'I'm staying with the family of Suzie, a friend of mine in Tel Aviv,' I said, confidently knowing they had open house for their daughter's friends.

When the train arrived in Paris, Debbie and I exchanged addresses and planned to meet again on the following day.

Suzie's mother welcomed me with kindness and hospitality. Visiting Paris at the same time was Suzie's brother, who made it his job to take Debbie and me to see the sights. The Eiffel Tower, the Louvre, Montmartre, the Tuilleries - all the places I had read about. I was intoxicated with the whole scene. We spent four days in Paris walking everywhere during daylight and dancing every evening.

The eleventh of June was my twentieth birthday. How wonderful to be spending it in Paris! That night, Debbie and I danced with a couple of tall, good-looking Nordic men, also visitors to Paris. I was bubbling over with enjoyment. After all I was leaving my teens behind. I was an experienced woman of the world!

In the interval we sat breathlessly down to a coffee when Debbie suddenly turned to both boys and said, 'Don't get any false ideas. She certainly likes dancing, and she's certainly very lively, but that's as far as it goes. Just remember, she's an innocent abroad!'

I was bemused. I had absolutely no idea anything could follow on from the good fun I was having.

At the end of the week Debbie and I parted in Paris, promising to meet up again in Tel Aviv.

*

My next step was to put myself in the hands of Imperial Airways to fly to Great Britain. It was extraordinary to walk on the soil of France, then to fly in the air over the Channel. I was thrilled to look down on the white cliffs of Dover.

'England!' I breathed to myself, as we landed at Croydon.

It was my dream coming true. I was determined to have a grand time, especially since here I could speak the language.

A coach drove passengers from the airport to various hotels. I was dropped off in the heart of London at the Regent Palace Hotel. By two I had unpacked my luggage and before I knew it the telephone in my room was ringing.

'Harriett, I'm downstairs waiting for you. I'm taking you out.' It was Phil, the middle-aged business man I had met in the Tel Aviv office and in whom I had confided my dream to visit London. As he had requested, I had cabled him my date of arrival.

Phil sat grinning in the back of his grey Rolls Royce.

'Welcome to London, Harriett,' he said cheerfully as the commissionaire opened the car door for me.

We were chauffeur driven up Regent Street, past Liberty's and round the back of Dickens & Jones to the London Palladium.

'Thought you would like a bit of London culture,' chuckled Phil. 'I've booked us in to the matinee to see Flanagan and Allen.'

I had never heard of them, but it felt grand sitting centre stalls enjoying a variety show. At last, Flanagan appeared on stage in his long racoon coat, grinning from ear to ear, while tall, serious-looking Allen fed him the stooge lines. They were top of the bill and exuded bonhomie and fun. The audience rose to them.

'Is that your dog? Does your dog have a family tree?' asked Allen.

'Nah! Any tree is good enough for my dog!' beamed Flanagan.

I thought they were uproariously funny and roared with the rest of the theatre.

Roaming, just roaming, in the cool of the evening air.' Flanagan sang melodiously, whilst Allen walked alongside him speaking the words. There was something so British about them. Especially when at the end of the show the audience and members of the cast stood to sing 'God Save the King.'

'What did you think of our boys?' asked Phil, as we made our way into the side street.

'I liked them very much,' I said, feeling overwhelmed. 'Morning in Paris, afternoon in London. I can hardly believe it!'

'Now, English tea in Argyle Street,' said Phil laughing at me. 'What would you like? Would you like toasted scones?'

I had never heard of toasted stones. I decided that as I'd never had them I would try the Toasted Stones! They turned out to be delicious.

'Thank you so much for a wonderful time,' I said as Phil dropped me back at the Regent Palace Hotel.

'My wife will be in touch to invite you to dinner this weekend,' he said. 'Enjoy London, Harriett!'

Back at the hotel I remembered my letters of introduction to Jack Sloane, the friend of a court judge in Tel Aviv, and to someone called Maurice. I made my way down to the foyer where I bought English stamps for the post. The tourist pamphlet looked inviting, so I immediately booked a tour of the city. Then feeling very pleased with myself, I lay on my bed listening to the sounds of the traffic outside and promptly fell into a deep sleep. That was my first day in London.

My second morning was spent on the tour. What a wonderful city! Buckingham Palace and the Mall, around to Westminster, Big Ben and the mother of Parliaments, up Whitehall to Trafalgar Square and the National Gallery, then along the Strand to the city for St. Paul's and the Tower, finally back along the Embankment beside the Thames, turning up to Charing Cross, Leicester Square and Piccadilly. I was thrilled with it all.

London was still decked out with flags from the Coronation in May. Excitement bubbled in the air. Store windows were decorated with pictures of King George VI with his Queen and two little princesses, Elizabeth and Margaret Rose.

Later that afternoon I wandered around Swan & Edgar, then up Regent Street. Everywhere displayed mementoes of the occasion. Liberty's seemed too posh a store to go in, so I walked on to Dickins & Jones, which was more my level. Here they sold the kind of underwear and makeup I was accustomed to. I did not buy anything, but I was having the most wonderful time just looking.

Early next morning Maurice telephoned in reply to my letter of introduction. He had a cultured English accent which I thought was cute. I happily made arrangements to meet him late that afternoon, but by four o'clock I was feeling extremely unwell. I had caught cold, my eyes were watering, my nose was stuffed up and I had a terrible headache. The change in climate must have disagreed with me. The last thing I wanted was to go out that evening. I took a bath, then lay supine on the bed, wrapped in my blue dressing gown, my hair in a towel.

The telephone made me jump when it rang. It was Maurice.

'I'm downstairs in the hotel,' he said. 'I'll wait for you by the desk.'

'I have a terrible cold,' I snuffled. 'I've just washed my hair, it is soaking wet - and I can't come out because I am in my dressing gown. I am sorry, another day.' I blew my nose for emphasis and was about to put the receiver down when I added for good measure, 'And men guests aren't allowed in my hotel room!'

That was that! I lay inert on top of the counterpane. A few minutes later I heard a knock on my door. I groaned and went to half open it, peering around. In the corridor stood a stranger, a tall, good-looking man with aquiline features, smartly dressed in a dark suit and tie.

'I'm Maurice,' he said, hovering at the door, then pushing it gently open.

'I told you I've got this awful cold. My hair is a mess,' I sniffed, pulling away the towel to show my wet tresses.

'It doesn't matter.'

I was not about to make an impression looking like that, but I felt too ill to care.

'*If the idiot wants to be here – that's fine! If he wants to see me looking ghastly, he can,*' I thought, knowing I was in no condition to impress any man.

'Well then, come in,' I said grudgingly.

He sat on the edge of the settee while I perched on my bed. My eyes were streaming and since I was quite near-sighted and far too vain to wear glasses, I wasn't sure if I would recognise him if we ever met again, which I doubted.

'Do you mind if I smoke?' he asked, offering me a Players. I shook my head.

'May I?' He hesitated.

I nodded. He lit up and sat back staring at me.

He hardly made introductory conversation. In fact he seemed to need someone to talk to and launched into his problems without preamble. I soon learned he was a Cambridge graduate, but was expected to work in the family business of clothing manufacturers.

'I hate it, but I feel obliged to run our factory as my father is very ill. I can't let the family business go downhill,' he confided. 'My heart is not in it.'

I made sympathetic noises, managing to interject a little about myself, but mainly I listened to him. Strangely, the more he talked the less I thought he was an idiot. He was educated, assured, knowledgeable and interesting, and I adored his accent. I thought it might be okay to meet him again.

He suddenly stood up saying, 'I have to leave.'

Was that it?

'You are quite something, Harriett,' he said, as he opened the door. 'Get better quickly. I am going to give you the time of your life!'

Then he was gone.

A huge bouquet of golden roses arrived outside my door next morning. In the attached envelope was a *love-letter* which began '*Dear Goldilocks*' and went on to say how much he was attracted to me. I realised that even in my sniffling state I was obviously the exact opposite of any girl he had ever met. I was an American, with a deep, throaty accent, emphasised by my cold! I supposed I was very desirable. It was fun, but I was not going to let it be important.

Jack contacted me that same evening.

'Hello Harriett, welcome to London. How are you?'

I told him through my sneezes.

'I'm coming to see you tomorrow anyway,' he said.

He was another respectable man who enjoyed showing a young woman around town in his smart car.

'You need fresh air,' he said, when he saw me. 'I know just the place to take you. Jump in.'

We drove out of the West End up the hill to Hampstead Heath. It was a soft warm day, the air clear. London lay spread out before me and I could pick out St. Paul's dome sparkling in the sunlight. As we walked around Kenwood I began to feel decidedly better.

'This is wonderful,' I breathed.

'I'll show you the Zoo,' he said, pleased at my enthusiasm.

I had never seen such a thing. Zoos were very unusual. I was intrigued to be so close to wild animals in cages. We ate ice-cream wafers as we leaned over the penguin pool at feeding time. Then we admired the apes.

'Who's watching who?' chuckled Jack, as he put a hand under my elbow. 'Time to go home!'

'Thank you for a wonderful day.' I shook Jack's hand by the hotel entrance.

'My family would like to meet you,' he said. 'I'll telephone to arrange dinner one night.'

When the telephone rang that evening I immediately picked it up and said, 'Hi, Jack!'

'Who's Jack?' It was Maurice.

'Oh, a friend,' I said casually.

'Look, I'm in the Territorial Army and they're having a Coronation Ball tomorrow night. If you are not busy, I would love to take you.' He paused at the end of the line.

I was surprised to feel a thrill of excitement.

'Fine,' I said.

This time, I was determined to make myself look as glamorous as possible. The sniffling Cinderella would be transformed into a princess.

He courteously held his car door open as I slid in the front beside him. We drove into the City of London where, over a sumptuous dinner, he introduced me to his friends and colleagues. It was an evening of pomp and ceremony, with loyal toasts to George VI and many grand but boring speeches. Afterwards, the band struck up for dancing. As we glided across the floor we seemed to blend together.

'*Wow!*' I thought.

Later, on the way back to the hotel, we talked incessantly to each other about anything and everything.

'You're just in time for the Coronation balls,' said Maurice as he dropped me off in the small hours. 'They seem to be going on forever, but now I know how much you like dancing I will have to take you out again.'

'You would anyway,' I said as a parting shot.

'Look,' he paused. 'Are you going out with anyone else? Are you busy this weekend?'

'I haven't made arrangements yet.'

'Actually, I can't get out of going to a house party this weekend. Maybe you could come with me. I will ask and let you know.'

'That would be just fine,' I said airily.

Who was I fooling? I thought he was the cat's whiskers - and he fancied me!

He rang the following night.

'Hello, Goldilocks. Are you recovered from the ball?'

'Sure,' I said.

He was making polite conversation but not saying anything, so I had to ask.

'Have your friends invited me to the house party this weekend?'

He did a double cough at the end of the line.

'I say, I am sorry,' he said. 'The problem is a bit awkward. One of them is my girlfriend.'

My heart sank, but I shrugged it off.

'That's okay,' I said gaily. I had boyfriends, plenty back home and many to entertain me in London. Who needed him?

'I'll spoil you when I get back,' he said.

Over the weekend, Jack took me to see a play called 'The Balalaika'. I was so excited because 'if one had not seen this musical, one had not lived!' I also visited Phil's home for dinner, so that I was properly busy and hardly thought of Maurice at all. At least I did not allow myself that luxury.

Happily, when he returned I was out. He left a message with the hotel reception for me to contact him. I was thinking about it when my room telephone rang.

'Hello, Goldilocks.'

'Maurice!' I tried to sound indifferent. 'Did you enjoy your weekend?'

He ignored the question.

'Look, I have a treat for you. I have tickets for Glyndebourne.'

'What's that?'

'An opera house in the country. Will you come with me?'

'I don't know much about opera,' I said. 'But it sounds okay.'

'I'll pick you up tomorrow at two o'clock,' he said. 'And be sure to wear your evening dress.'

'You're kidding! In the afternoon?' I roared with laughter. 'You English are so quaint.'

We took a taxi to the station to catch the Glyndebourne special. All the passengers were elegantly attired in evening dress. Maurice looked wonderfully debonair and I felt quite a catch. We had tea on the train. I ordered toasted scones with confidence.

At Lewes, we were coached to the large country estate which housed its own opera theatre. On that summer's evening, the gardens were scented with blossoms and freshly mown lawns where the audience could walk whilst waiting for the performance. The opera was by Mozart, but as I knew little about the music it was inconsequential to me. On the other hand the setting was magnificent. During the interval, which lasted for over an hour, Maurice wined and dined me in the restaurant whilst other visitors sat in the grounds with picnic baskets from Fortnum & Masons. The whole experience was magical, like nothing I had ever imagined.

Later, whilst waiting at the railway station, the damp chilly haze of the July evening made me shiver. Maurice kept his arm around me until we arrived in London in the small hours and taxied to my hotel.

'Come out with me tomorrow,' he said.

'Today? Sure.' I grinned. 'But let me sleep until seven!'

The weather was glorious when he drove me to Cambridge. We went punting on the River Cam. It was extraordinary to see The Backs and colleges from the water side. He pointed out his old haunts when he had been an undergraduate. College term was finished but there were several undergraduates roaming about whom he eyed wistfully.

'I still miss the University,' he said.

'You have hardly been away long. Only a year or two.'

'Harriett. I am much older than you think. I am twenty-eight.'

I grinned at him. 'That's all right. I prefer mature men.'

During the rest of my stay, he took me out many times. We went to the National Gallery, the Victoria and Albert Museum, the Tower, St. Paul's Cathedral and numerous venues of interest. We danced in famous night-clubs. One called 'The Thatched Barn' was out on the open road away from London.

I had thought that by now I was a sophisticated woman of the world. After all I had come from the States. I had toured Europe. I lived in Palestine. But nothing could have prepared me for the wonderful time I was having in London with Maurice.

'When will I see your home and meet your family?' I asked eventually. 'I would like to do so before I leave.'

'Harriett, I don't live with my family. I share a house with my girlfriend and a couple of other friends.'

I gasped with astonishment. I had had no idea. I could not imagine what he had told his girlfriend about me. It made me do a double think about Maurice.

On the morning of my departure, he turned up at my hotel just as I was about to board the Imperial Airways coach.

'Goodbye, Goldilocks dearest,' he said, taking me in his arms. 'I will see you again. I won't forget you. Please write.'

He looked crestfallen as I boarded. I leaned out of the coach window above him. He suddenly seemed like a vulnerable kid who needed looking after. I do not know why but I said, 'You are very smart - but your shoes aren't polished! And you know you need a haircut!'

That was my parting shot in the middle of the day as the coach pulled away from the Regent Palace Hotel, London.

*

Travelling was so exciting, I hardly had time to feel any emotion except that I was on my way home. There was no direct flight. The plane flew across Europe on short hauls, stopping after a number of hours to re-fuel. Each evening the plane landed at about seven or eight o'clock, when passengers were given a meal in a nearby hotel and a room for the night. At 3 o'clock in the morning, we were woken up to have breakfast before we boarded to fly off again.

I had not prepared for an extended trip. On the second night I rinsed out my underwear, but was dismayed to find it still damp when we were awakened. After that I had to put up with feeling grubby. I made a vow that I would carry fresh underwear and a clean blouse in my hand luggage whenever I travelled in future.

Imperial Airways flew to Egypt, from where I made my way home to Herzlia. My family were overjoyed to have me safely home. They had already received several of my letters, which travelled very quickly. I had written one letter home with particular feeling which my mother kept in her pocket.

It read: *'Thank you both for my upbringing. I have been entertained in many Jewish homes over here (with more religion, or less, than ours) but I always felt comfortable everywhere. I wanted you to know how grateful I am for everything you have given me.'*

I could hardly stop talking about my adventures. Sol and Esther asked dozens of questions and my parents were keen to know more.

Esther suddenly interrupted the flow of conversation.

'You wrote you were taken out by Maurice. What's he like?' she asked.

I could hardly assess what I felt for him, except that he was like no-one I had ever met before.

I hesitated. He was difficult to describe.

'He's English,' I said.

CHAPTER 12

Palestine (1937)

The holiday of a lifetime was over. It was wonderful to be re-united with my family. Sol had come home from training especially to see me. We were together, exchanging stories of what happened since we last met. It was like old times of family reunions back in the States, but there was heartache that my older sisters were so far away. I silently resolved that if ever I had children, I would make sure my family stayed together and were never broken up.

The following morning, I collected another letter from Maurice. I read it through a dozen times, unable to get my feelings straight. I wanted to set my thoughts down for him, so planned to sit under the pomegranate tree to write my reply. Before that, I conscientiously used the public telephone to speak to the Tel Aviv office where the boss, Mr. Seligman, inquired if I was back safely in Herzlia.

'I would appreciate a few days with my parents,' I replied, tentatively suggesting I would return to the office on Monday.

Max Seligman spluttered loudly, then barked down the wire, 'Come immediately!'

It was good to be needed, but not that good. I had to take the next bus to Tel Aviv, where I reached my apartment at two thirty, dumped my luggage and rushed to the office. I entered the boss's office without knocking.

'Mr. Seligman, you've not given me even a minute to unpack. What's so urgent?'

He sat back, smiling with relief.

'Harriett my dear, I need you. Your replacement is an absolute flop. Work has just piled up waiting for you. Besides, I leave for Europe on Friday.' He looked rather sheepish. 'And I need you to sort important papers that I must take regarding London clients.'

What was it about men? They seemed so educated, so self-contained, but they crumpled when organising simple things.

The rest of the afternoon was spent trying to sort out the jumbled mess of paperwork to be tackled later and filling his briefcase with the correct papers. By the time I was at my own desk I was feeling distinctly drained.

'All done? Good!' said Mr. Seligman cheerfully. 'What would I do without you, Harriett? Let me take you out for dinner.'

Dinner turned out to be an office farewell party for him, combined with a welcome home party for me! Everyone surrounded me with eager questions. It was all too much. Soon I was hardly able to stand up straight.

'Are you all right?' Max Seligman looked anxiously at me as I swayed unsteadily on my feet.

'I have a terrific headache. It's tiredness.'

'You need rest,' said Arnold, coming to my rescue. 'I'll take you home.'

I fell into a deep sleep almost at once, but later in the night I dreamt I was in London again. I woke feeling much better but wondering where on earth I was.

Next morning I arrived at the office to start on the enormous backlog, resigned to hours of extra work. At eleven, Joe, a friend of Mr. Seligman, arrived to drive him to the station for the train to Haifa. That was a relief. At least the boss would be out of the way.

'Have a good journey.' I waved over the typewriter.

'Thank you, Harriett,' said my boss. 'But I need you to come along to the station. I want to dictate to you. You have no idea how I have missed you. Hurry up, I am late.'

I grabbed my notepad and pencil and followed him into the back of the car where he immediately started to dictate letters. He must have been carrying the information around in his head all week because words streamed out of him with hardly a pause. I was hard pressed to keep the notebook steady on my knees, let alone write clearly in the moving car. I felt decidedly travel sick. We reached the station in time to see the rear end of the train pulling away from the platform.

'If we step on it we can catch it at Hadera,' said Joe. He pressed the accelerator and we drove full speed out of Tel Aviv on the road to Haifa.

All of a sudden there was a loud bang, the car swerved to the left and came to an abrupt halt. For one horrible moment I thought we had been attacked by an Arab gang. Cars were often targeted by brigands lying in wait beside the road. My life flashed before me as Joe turned off the engine to get out.

'Stay in the car!' he shouted.

Relief flooded back when he exclaimed, 'Puncture! I'll have to change the tyre. Max, get out the jack.'

By the time the two men had succeeded, it was too late to catch the train, so we had no alternative but to drive on to Haifa.

'Just as well the boat does not leave until this evening,' said Max Seligman, adopting a resigned air and making jokes to relieve the tension.

We piled into the car again only to have another puncture, with the same heart-stopping panic, a mile up the road. When we eventually reached Haifa docks it was after five. I felt pale and ill from the journey. Max Seligman did not seem to notice but waved cheerily as he lifted his luggage from the boot, shouting his final instructions.

'I leave the running of the office to you, Harriett, until I get back. All right?'

I opened my mouth to protest but my boss had turned and disappeared into the port.

Joe laughed at my look of horror.

'Cheer up! Max told me he has every faith in you.'

My head was spinning. I could hardly think straight, let alone run an office

'I can't face going back tonight. I have friends in Haifa. I'll call and surprise them,' I said.'

I asked Joe to drop me off outside a terraced apartment, from where sounds of merriment drifted down. When I entered, everybody surrounded me in surprise. I had unintentionally walked in on a party and found many of my friends there, including Yona.

'We thought you were in London!' they exclaimed.

'How was it?' asked Yona, kissing me on the cheek but not wanting an answer.

'Wonderful!' I breathed, sinking into a chair.

Everyone inundated me with questions about my trip. After an hour I was so exhausted I begged a bed for the night. Making my excuses to everyone I lay down and sank into a dreamless sleep.

Early next morning, while the household was quiet, I rose to catch the train back to Tel Aviv, arriving at the office by nine and worked solidly through until three.

'Thank goodness it's Friday,' I sighed, as I made my way back to Herzlia in time for Shabbat.

As the sun began to fade, I sat on my bed recounting the day in my letter to Maurice until Papa called that Shabbat was nearly here and that I should put away my writing for another time.

The subsequent weeks went from bad to worse. In Max Seligman's absence, the business had bursts of hectic activity when I could hardly cope, followed by hours of boredom that I filled by typing copious gossipy letters to Mildred in the States and Maurice in England. The heat was oppressive and everyone's temper was frayed, including mine.

The harvest on father's small-holding was not good either. I worried about the health of my parents. They both looked so weary and aged. Sol, who was only there part-time, argued constantly with J.L. about farming methods, the new versus the old. I realized that since crops were failing, money was becoming a problem. I did not know what I could do except offer to help with money, but they refused to take it.

I spent Rosh Hashanah, the Jewish New Year, at home with my family, but the festival was tinged with sadness at the news that Mildred had died. Someone so young and lovely had gone forever. It made my family even more precious to me.

*

The political situation had calmed down at the start of the year while Palestine awaited the outcome of the Peel Commission. In July the Commission recommended considering partition of the land. The Arabs immediately denounced the scheme, as did the Zionists. Now the situation was worsening. Attacks increased against Jews, who retaliated. To try to maintain the peace, curfews were imposed by the British authorities. The old prison fort at Acre now held captive both Arabs and Jews.

In September, two British officials were shot dead in Nazareth by Arabs. Five Arab leaders were arrested and deported. The Mufti of Jerusalem was deprived of office, but escaped to Damascus to organize revolt.

Now many young men from the Haganah, originally trained to defend Jewish settlements, joined the Palestine Police to help combat the Arab gangs who were attacking transport, pipe-lines, railways, even fields and orchards.

My mother seemed more worried about me than usual. For the first time she expressed concern when I had to return to the office before Yom Kippur.

'I will be fine,' I assured her. 'Tel Aviv is a Jewish city. We can take care of ourselves. I am more concerned about you out here.'

J.L. tutted. 'They don't attack at weekends,' he said. 'At night we have our boys guarding us.'

He looked over at Sol, who was tired out and dozing in a chair. Sol had joined Orde Wingate's Night Squads training to go on the offensive. These days he was often away from the farm. He never spoke of his experiences and we did not ask him, although I told him that if he was ever short of money to come to me.

He nodded. 'I may need more help than money from you, Harriett. You work for Max Seligman, don't you? He has a good reputation for defending our boys if they get into trouble.'

We all knew what would happen to Sol if he were ambushed by Arabs, or caught by the British. The family were increasingly worried for him, including those in the States who kept writing that we should return. They were aware, as were we all, of the bleak situation for Jews in Nazi Germany.

In Palestine the British had curtailed Jewish immigration to appease the Arabs. All the same, illegal beach landings were still causing them problems. Mounted guards on full alert frequently patrolled our nearest beaches so that my days as decoy were over. But further along the coast, silent, stealthy figures made sure refugees were being safely landed and transported into the homes of waiting friends.

In my own social world, little drama touched my consciousness at first, but gradually I was coming to understand the enormity of my father's dream and the nature of our struggle to achieve it.

*

Almost from the moment we arrived in Palestine, Esther had a boy friend, Mattie. He had called to say 'hello', as did many immigrants from the States. It so happened he was the son of an old friend of J.L. who had dangled Esther on his knee when she was a baby. It seemed natural that Mattie and Esther should hit it off immediately, even though she was only fifteen at the time and he was five years older. There was never any question of him taking advantage of Esther but they retained a wonderfully close friendship through the next three years. J.L. was cautious about giving his blessing, especially since they were so young.

'Now Esther,' J.L. said, sitting back in his chair. 'How do you know you really love Mattie?'

Esther smiled to herself.

'Well, I like being with him.' She paused, then added shyly, 'I like it when he kisses me.'

'Have you ever kissed anyone else?' queried Papa.

'No.'

'So how do you know that you like it if *he* kisses you? You never kissed anyone else!' Papa was serious. 'Suppose you marry him, then in a year's time some man comes up and kisses you and you say 'Oh, this is nice, I like this!' That's not good, is it?'

Esther looked confused.

Papa continued. 'I want you not to see Mattie for six months. I want you to go out with other people. If at the end of that time you still think he's the one you like, then you can marry him.'

Esther pulled in a deep sigh, but had to agree. By now she had left school, so that her whole world was changing once more.

'I want you to stay in Tel Aviv with Harriett,' Papa told her. My kid sister brightened visibly.

'Okay!' she said cheerfully. 'I'll find a job there.'

My father turned to me with his instructions.

'You are going to house her. She and Mattie are not going to meet for six months. Is that understood?'

Esther and I nodded, then went to our bedroom to decide what clothes she should bring.

Next week there was hard work in the office for me. Esther spent time searching for an office job. She eventually found one in a local bank, starting the following Monday. I heaved a sigh of relief that this should keep her out of trouble. I did not really want to be in charge of my kid sister anymore.

Esther's love life was on hold for the moment, but my social life was as busy as ever. Esther and I returned to Herzlia for weekends, so our parents were pleased that everything was going to plan, or so they thought.

On my way home one evening from the office, I caught sight of Esther and Mattie standing on the corner talking to each other. This was not the first time and I lost my temper.

'You're breaking your promise!' I exclaimed, walking over to break up the liaison

Next evening when I returned home, there was Mattie in my apartment with Esther. I was furious, especially since the responsibility to keep them apart had devolved on me. By Friday I was neurotic about her.

'Papa says you have to see other people, so I've made a date for you this Sunday with Walter, while I go to the cinema. He's a real nice fellow.'

'Do I have to?' My kid sister was really obstinate.

'You have to,' I insisted.

'I don't think it is a good idea,' said Esther. 'You'll be sorry.'

'The office is where I *am* wanted,' I thought next morning as I opened the post. The telephone rang.

'Mr. Seligman's office,' I answered.

'Harriett? This is Walter.'

'Hi, Walter.'

'You've got a crazy sister!'

'What's the matter with my sister?'

'She hit me!'

'What do you mean, she hit you?'

'I kissed her. She slapped my face!'

I snorted. 'You are right. I've got a crazy sister!'

I thought, '*Wait till I get hold of her!*'

Esther was completely nonplused when I exploded.

'You go out with a boy and you slap him!'

'Well, I didn't want him to kiss me.'

'That's it!'

When I saw my father next weekend I raged.

'Papa, you must listen to me. If you want to keep Esther away from Mattie, then you do it! I am having nothing further to do with her. Every time I walk in the street I see them together. He even visits her in the apartment!'

It was a fait accompli. Esther had her way.

'They are getting married,' said our father emphatically.

'Thank you, Papa!' said Esther delightedly. 'I promise you that Mattie and I will be very happy together.'

The Gold Family. Minsk c. 1906

Left: My parents on their engagement
Minsk 1906

The Meltzer Family.
Minsk c. 1912

My parents,
Herzlia,
Israel 1974

The 'sisters'
Left to right:
Rhea, Harriett, Leah
Esther and Rose.

Tel Binyamin 1937.
On the occasion of
the wedding of my
dearest friend, Phyllis.

Outside our House
in Herzlia, 1936
Esther, Mama and myself
with Mildred kneeling
in front.

Terrace at the Ritz Hotel,
Tel Aviv, 1935.
The beaches were crowded
even then.

כל אדם משתמש EVERYBODY USES

Mildred and I sitting on
Mattie's motorcycle, 1936

In Achad Ha'am Street,
July 1937

The Opera House,
Tel Aviv, 1935

Publicity card for 'Egged' taxis, 1935

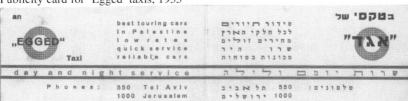

an
"EGGED"
Taxi

best touring cars
in Palestine
low rates
quick service
reliable cars

day and night service

Phones: 550 Tel Aviv
         1000 Jerusalem

בטקס' של
"אגד"

סידור תיורים
לכל חלקי הארץ
מחירים זולים
שרות מהיר
מכונות בטוחות

שרות יומם ולילה

טלפונים: 550 תל אביב
          1000 ירושלים

Yona and I at the Midsummer Ball.
San Remo Hotel, Tel Aviv, 1937.

Among the first orange crop of 1938. I am in my Harris tweed suit made from
material sent by Maurice.

First wedding anniversary of Phyllis (far right) and Yadin (back centre).

THE MANCHESTER GUARDIAN,

TUESDAY, FEBRUARY 8, 1938

JEW NOT TO DIE

Sentence of Death Commuted

JERUSALEM, FEBRUARY 7.
By decision of the General Officer Commanding it was announced to-night that the sentence of death on Ezekiel Altman, a 22-year-old Jewish super-numerary constable, has been commuted to life imprisonment.

Altman, the first Jew to be sentenced to death by the special military courts, was found guilty of firing at an Arab omnibus, near Jerusalem, on December 27. The trial lasted three days. Altman was defended by Mr. Max Seligman, a former Cardiff man. A plea for clemency was made on Saturday by Dr. Isaac Herzog, the Chief Rabbi, formerly of Dublin.

An Arab youth of 17, named Mohammed Deeb Irsheid, was sentenced yesterday by the Jerusalem military court to ten years' imprisonment for carrying a Mills bomb. He was arrested on January 29 for loitering in a suspicious manner near the middle-class Jewish suburb of Rehavia.—Reuter.

Portrait of my boss, Max Seligman.

THE PALESTINE POST

Headlines from The Palestine Post.

JERUSALEM   VOL. XIV. No. 3767.   PRICE 10 MILS.

MASSACRE IN TIBERIAS TOWN
NINETEEN JEWS KILLED; 3 WOUNDED IN NIGHT ATTACK

PAGE TWO

SELIGMAN'S EVIDENCE IN OWN DEFENCE

PAGE TWO

SELIGMAN CASE OPENS IN JERUSALEM
Twenty-One Counts in Connection with Illegal Immigration

Before Judge Curry and Acting Judge Elias Khoury in the Jerusalem District Court yesterday morning the trial of Max Seligman on twenty-one counts connected with illegal immigration was begun.

Mr. M. Eliash, who appeared for the accused, assisted by Mr. A. Levitsky, raised an objection to the jurisdiction of the Court before the accused pleaded. The Court, however, after hearing Crown Counsel in reply, held that it had jurisdiction. The accused then pleaded Not Guilty on all the counts.

Seligman Sentenced to Six Months

Lydda Airfield, 1 April 1940.
Back row: Sol, Papa,
Mamma, Mattie.
In front: Me and Esther.
On the back is written
'Saying Goodbye'.

Standing behind our house
looking towards Herzlia, 1937.
The land Papa said would one
day be covered by villas and
Hotels.

Extract of letter from Maurice

My wedding day. Grosvenor House Hotel, London, 17 April 1940.

CHAPTER 13

Acre and Jerusalem (1938)

The situation for Jews was worsening, especially in Nazi Germany. In Palestine the Irgun Zvi Leumi, the Jewish People's Army, set out to defend themselves against Arab attacks. They began to capture arms and ammunition from the British and secretly train underground soldiers to fend off the gangs who came across the border at night, attacking and killing Jews. Many moderate Jews, who favoured co-operation with the British, considered the Irgun to be terrorists. It caused a great political schism within the Jewish community. The Haganah wanted to do everything by peaceful methods. The Irgun wanted to force the situation because they said we were running out of time. I do not think J.L. agreed with their methods, but he certainly supported their cause.

He held his counsel when Sol was around except to say, 'Woe betide any of you boys if you are captured.'

'Don't worry, Papa,' said Sol reassuringly. 'We know what we are doing.'

Sol knew that the Palestine Police were vigilantly imposing constant curfews and house searches, trying to prevent ambushes and incidents. Occasionally they were successful in catching our boys red-handed with illegal arms. Some of Sol's friends had been captured holding the booty. They could hardly deny they were 'liberating' guns and ammunition from the British to help their own cause.

'The British know they are sitting on a powder keg with a jumping jack nearby,' said Sol. 'I suppose they have no option but to stamp on us.'

He was right. The Mandate meted out harsh sentences to our boys simply because they were known members of the Irgun Zvi Leumi.

My boss, Max Seligman, was particularly in demand to defend Jewish prisoners brought before the British Military Courts. Max was a British Jew, a lawyer and a Zionist. His great sense of humour, with his outstanding ability to clarify issues, confounded the prosecution. He frequently won lighter sentences for his clients, as in the case of one young man accused of possessing batches of illegal Irgun propaganda leaflets in his apartment. The police insisted that he was about to distribute them. Max pleaded that the defendant had assured him they were being stored merely for use as toilet paper, of which there was a shortage.

Everyone in court laughed aloud and the defendant walked free.

'Only Max could have thought of that one!' we said proudly.

*

In January 1938, I once again found myself in the back of a car with Max on the road to Haifa. This time we circumvented the port and drove further to the imposing grey crusader fort at Acre. It was an impregnable fortress, having resisted invaders and withstood bombardment for centuries. Today, British soldiers manned the huge wooden doors which swung open for us to enter. Enclosed within was the sombre prison for both Arab and Jewish miscreants. An officer greeted us politely, then walked us across the courtyard to a barred room where we awaited our client, the prisoner Altman.

'Take notes, Harriett. I want to be clear about his defence,' Max told me, as a good-looking young man was brought in by the guards. Max indicated that we should be left alone with the prisoner, so they withdrew. Then Mr. Seligman introduced me and himself, adding that he wanted full and frank details of the case. Altman smiled, then told his story for me to take down.

Ezekial Altman was one of the boys who had joined the British auxiliary police, but who secretly trained with the Betar (an off-shoot of Irgun) in a quarry near Kiryat Anavim. Last winter Arab gangs attacked Kiryat Anavim, killing at least five Jews. Our boys were fuming. In retaliation, Altman took a strategic position near the highway and shot at an Arab omnibus before returning to report the incident to his commanding officer. He was arrested next morning.

In the cell Max warned him not to plead politics in defence. Altman readily agreed to accept sole responsibility for his actions so as not to implicate any members of the Betar. However, since he had admitted the offence to the authorities, he realised he would have a sentence imposed on him.

'I'll see what I can do to alleviate it,' Max told him.

We shook hands and said goodbye. Max was unusually silent in the taxi taking us back to Tel Aviv.

On an early February morning, I accompanied Mr. Seligman and junior counsel in a car speeding along the dangerous road to Jerusalem. The air was fresh and clear, all was quiet. The golden city stood serene on the hills, reflecting sparkles of light from the morning sun. I felt a sense of pride and awe that this was our Holy City.

We arrived safely at the small hotel where we were to stay during Altman's trial. I deposited my hand luggage in my bedroom, from where I could hear the sounds of the city bustling outside. I had been given half an hour to tidy up, gather my papers and notes, then make my way to the court.

The trial of Ezekial Altman began on 2nd February, 1938. I sat in the Military courtroom behind Max, noting down the procedures of the trial, the indictment and the hearing.

Max made an emotional appeal in mitigation. I learned then what a fine speaker he was and why he was exceptional in dealing with judges to minimise sentences. I was exhausted by early evening and went straight to bed.

Next morning at breakfast I noticed to my surprise that some members of the court were also staying at the hotel and nodded to me. But even more to my surprise was a lady whom I recognised as Henrietta Szold, an old friend of my parents, who had often visited our house in New Haven. These days she was a woman of great importance in the Zionist movement. I sat gingerly at her table and introduced myself.

'Harriett!' she exclaimed delightedly. 'Whatever are you doing here? When I last saw you, you were at school in bobby socks.'

It was good to have someone to talk to, someone who remembered the old days, someone who had a sympathetic ear. I did not feel so alone.

The trial lasted three days. Finally, we awaited the verdict. When the judge returned he placed a black cloth on his head and pronounced that Altman be sentenced to hang. We were horrified. It was the first time capital punishment had been meted out to a Jew by the British.

Altman stood tall and steadfast in the dock and started to sing the Hatikvah. Immediately Max and I, and any Jew present, rose to attention, our hearts heavy but our morale high.

'Mr.Seligman, I protest at your standing while the prisoner sings,' admonished the judge.

'I always stand for my National Anthem,' replied Max, calmly sitting down at the finish.

The judge seemed embarrassed.

Mr. Seligman looked devastated.

'I have to stop this travesty,' he said to me. 'When the court adjourns I am going to judges' chambers to lodge an appeal. Meanwhile, get my office to inform the Jewish Agency, the Chief Rabbi, the newspapers, anyone you can think of to put pressure on the court verdict.'

Altman was stalwart in accepting his fate, but the whole of the Jewish community, in Palestine and abroad, was aghast that his life should be taken from him by order of a British court. Representation to the British government was intense. We were persistent and hopeful, but never certain of success.

Imagine our relief when three days later the Manchester Guardian officially reported: 'Jew not to Die. By decision of the General Officer Commanding it was announced tonight that the sentence of death on Ezekial Altman, a 22 year old Jewish auxiliary constable, has been commuted to life imprisonment.'

Max had pulled it off.

'To save a life is to save the world entire.' I quoted to an exhausted Max Seligman back in his office.

'He will live to fight another day,' prophesied my boss.

That weekend, I returned to Herzlia feeling elated, ready to tell my parents all about the trial and my breakfasts with their old friend, Henrietta Szold.

*

Maurice and I exchanged dozens of letters, sometimes four or five a month. I wrote to him about the Altman case and how my boss was being highly praised for his excellent defence and pleading. He wrote how much he thought of me, how I should take care of myself (he never added 'for me'). We held conversations on paper across the seas. My letters fell into an off-hand manner because if I tried to write differently it just spoilt whatever I wanted to say. I was too forthright! What I thought of writing never sounded or looked the same on paper. So I wrote him long chatty letters, similar to the ones I had sent to Mildred.

'I have to admit that you have a marvellously clear trend of thought and set your arguments out well,' I praised him. But he also expressed forceful views on life which often I did not agree with and wrote him so.

It was a strange sort of arguing, putting opinions in a letter and waiting for a written reaction. Often he would write back, 'You are right, Harriett.' But on some things he was intransigent. He felt the laws of Judaism should be properly observed. I happened to mention that last autumn some people in Tel Aviv did not fast on Yom Kippur, and that one of my friends even held a party on the day. I did not believe they should have behaved so, but it was not for me to condemn them. Maurice on the other hand expressed horror, disbelief and censure, as if he were a rabbi.

As to the political situation in Palestine, he did not have any understanding of what we were going through. Naturally he was sympathetic to the British government. I pointed out that the Anschluss in Austria on 12th March 1938, boded ill for any Jew living under the new Nazi regime. I reiterated sarcastically that all the British authorities managed to do in Palestine was announce an immigration quota *reduced* to only three thousand Jews over the next six months. It was evident to me 'that the English government must show the Arabs that they are in sympathy'. And I did not care too much what he thought, he was wrong. We were quarrelling on paper.

I suppose I should not have been surprised when his letters stopped, but I was. Well, if he took umbrage, so what! I refrained from writing to him and concentrated on other, more important matters.

Yona had asked me to marry him. It was flattering. I knew I would never marry such a playboy, but it was fun to string him along anyway.

'Let's go home to my mother and father and if they approve I will marry you,' I said, knowing I was pretty safe.

My parents were smart people. They knew if I had really wanted it I would never have gone back to ask them. We drove that very evening to Herzlia, arriving in time for a meal. My parents were gracious and charming, making us very welcome. After dinner, J.L. and Yona sat back with a brandy.

'Mr. Gold, Harriett is quite a girl,' Yona started. 'I would like to marry her. She's beautiful, she's got spirit, she's not like any other girl.'

My father feigned surprise.

'And what do you think about love?' he asked philosophically.

Yona cleared his throat. 'That depends what you mean by love.'

J.L. roared with laughter. 'If a man does not know what love is he is not the husband for my girl!'

I knew that without saying anything I could rely on J.L. and he would sort out the matter for me. We were teasing Yona and tying him into little knots.

'I'm sorry, Yona,' I said, looking very downcast. 'I can't marry you without my father's permission, and he's given you the thumbs down!'

In the meantime, Gaby had encouraged me to join the Charity Committee to raise money for good causes. There were many deserving families struggling for a foothold in their new country. There were widows, bereaved from Arab attacks on their men folk. Mothers without sons. We could always find somewhere for the money to go. The difficulty was in raising it from the more affluent members of our society.

'Tel Aviv is a concrete city,' said Gaby to the group at one meeting. 'Kids wander about in the streets after school. Apart from the beach, there are no parks or safe places for them to play. I propose we have a special project to raise money for a children's playground.'

We all thought that was a first-rate idea and set about organising collections. But the response was surprisingly poor.

'Who wants to give money for other people's children to play?' they argued.

'Only people with children might, but then they are struggling to keep the kids fed and clothed,' I said. 'But I think I have an idea that might work.'

Next day I composed a letter asking for donations and wrote to all the unmarried men I knew, including Mac and Yona, adding the postscript:

'Who knows, one of the children running around in the playground may be yours!'

I suppose it was a way of getting my own back. It was an outrageous suggestion, but it worked. Almost by return of post large donations came rolling in and I collected more than anyone else.

'I knew you would be an asset the minute I saw you,' said Gaby delightedly.

CHAPTER 14

Tel Aviv and Acre (1938)

Married life was boring Ida, whose job I had moved into. She asked to return to the office. Mr. Seligman agreed, although I knew there was not enough work for the two of us. Immediately I found that I was no longer involved in the important legal work, but given everyday contracts. Ida had come right back in and taken over. I was highly aggrieved, especially since I was always being offered better jobs with larger salaries to lure me away from the firm. I knew I was good. When a client banker offered me a job working five days a week, seven till two, at a wage of £20 a month, I decided to accept.

'Right! I'm off!' I said.'

Max Seligman was engrossed in a legal tome when I knocked on his door and entered his office. Smoke rose from the ashtray in a thin curl. Legal papers covered his desk and a tidy pile of legal books stood on the floor beside his chair.

'Harriett?' he said without looking up.

I waited fuming, holding a pile of typed documents for a good two seconds.

'Right, this is it,' I exclaimed. 'I've had enough of this lot! I'm off to another, better job.'

I banged the papers down on to his desk.

Max sat back, calmly picked up his cigarette and repeated my name with a smile.

'I'm not going to be relegated by Ida to this kind of work. I've been bothered long enough by other people who want me for their offices. Better hours and better wages.' I stopped, realising that I had lost my temper in front of my boss.

'I'm sorry,' I stammered.

'Harriett.' This time his voice was placating. 'You know I can't do without you. Calm down. I'll deal with it.'

He kept his word. By the end of the week Ida had gone and I was in complete charge of the office with an increased salary.

The first thing I did was organise an office change around. The reception room in the centre led to the offices of the senior staff, and from there through a corridor to other lawyers and clerks, then into a staffroom for secretaries and typists. I organised essential refurbishing, ordered stationery, and became office administrator. From that time on, staff had to come to me for everything. If they wanted to see the boss; or if they wanted a day off, or ran out of stationery, I dealt with it, making sure everything ran smoothly. I realised I had the good fortune to work in an office which was well-known, where I met and often became friendly with many people of importance. So I felt proud that I kept that office together. I suppose for the first time in my life I knew what it was like to be in charge and I made sure it was done properly.

My father thought that was perfectly normal. He never said to me, 'Aren't you a clever girl?' But I knew he was proud of me. Except for one thing. One evening in Herzlia he suddenly turned to me.

'Have you got a cigarette?' he asked.

'Yes,' I replied immediately out of habit. I handed him a Players before I remembered that I had never seen him smoke. He shook his head and pushed my offer away.

'How did you know I smoked?' I said.

'My friend, Mr. Bender, saw you smoking in the office.'

He never said 'You shouldn't smoke. Why do you smoke?' He just let me know he knew, and that really he disapproved.

*

I loved living and working in Tel Aviv. I was thoroughly involved in the hectic social life that is part of every city. Also, since my parents had been involved in the Zionist Movement for the development of a Jewish Homeland, it was my good fortune that I had met many people in the States who were now actively working in Palestine.

Surprisingly, we were on very friendly terms with the British even though they held the Mandate. My friends often threw parties especially to meet and entertain them. At one of these affairs where the company was well dressed, intellectual and amusing, I was introduced to a young married couple. He was a slightly built officer in the British army, whose reputation for bravery had preceded him. He was Orde Wingate, with his dark-haired, beautiful wife, Lorna. I felt honoured to meet them and shook their hands warmly. He was training our boys off the cuff to go on the offensive against marauding Arabs. I knew Sol served under him. We were all happy he was here doing such vital work and we loved him for it. He had a deep Christian belief that Jews had the right to return to the Holy Land. As a bible-loving man, and appreciating that Christianity was born out of Judaism, he firmly believed in the adage *'If I forget thee, oh Jerusalem, may my right hand forget its cunning.'* His faith supported him in training our boys.

Next morning, I sent money to Sol stationed in Hanita with the Night Squads. I cared deeply for him and knew he could do with the cash from his kid sister.

Even though the death penalty on Altman had been commuted, we were aware that our boys were in ever present danger, either from Arab reprisals or from the vigilance of the Palestine Police. A section of the Irgun underground movement was Betar, composed mainly of young Eastern European Jews who had managed to get to Palestine against all odds.

As the gathering momentum of Nazi persecution took its hold in Europe more Jews than ever were 'knocking at the door' and more Jews than ever were being turned down by the British.

The boys in Betar felt they had nothing left to lose. They were ready, heart and soul, to die for a Jewish Homeland. If they were caught they were warned not to name Max Seligman as their lawyer, but to plead innocence of all legal matters. However, if they were charged with a serious offence, then they could use this man who had gained a reputation for defending them with great ability and heartfelt fervour.

So it was that in the late spring of 1938, after Arabs had attacked and killed several Jews in the area of Rosh Pinah, three Betar boys laid ambush to an Arab bus in retaliation. But their plan failed and they were caught. Max Seligman was asked to defend them.

This time the boss and I were driven with an army escort through the Arab town to the sombre fort at Acre. Even though the climate was hot and humid, I shivered as we passed through the wooden doors into the inner courtyard. There was a chill sense of foreboding, linked with the noises of the prisoners and the clanging of doors.

Again, we were received politely by a British officer, then led through dark corridors to an interview room where we awaited the prisoners. They were brought in separately, each

138

being able to talk freely to us but not to each other. Their stories were the same.

They had had enough of Arab raids against defenceless Jews. It was time for retaliation and attack. This time they had not succeeded, but they assured us that when they were at liberty they would try again.

'We will not give up until we have a Jewish Homeland, a State of our own. Nowhere else will we be free,' said the eldest of the three, Shlomo Ben Yosef, a swarthy young man from Eastern Europe.

In Palestine, to my ear, everyone had an accent except the Americans, but his accent was especially difficult to understand. I had great difficulty in jotting down my shorthand. It was so important to get a true record of what was said that every so often I read it back for him to agree.

In his homeland, he had seen Jews being rounded up and shot. He knew that because of atrocities carried out by the Nazis in Germany and Eastern Europe, time was running out for Jews everywhere. A Jewish homeland was needed *now*, and he was prepared to die for it.

Mr. Seligman was courteous and appreciative throughout the interviews, and when we sank exhaustedly into the back of the car to return to the office, he thanked me.

'Type your notes as soon as you can for me as a basis for their defence,' he said. Then he fell silent for a while before adding, 'We may face difficulties.'

*

A letter from Maurice awaited me on my return that evening. To my astonishment he said that *since he had been engaged* he had not been able to write his true feelings for me, but now that the engagement was *off* he would like to see me again. As it was soon to be my birthday, he would send me a three months ticket to London. What cheek! I was outraged that all this time he had lied to me about his life. He had had a fiancée. I could hardly credit it. And now he expected me to halt my life in Tel Aviv, up sticks and go over to him!

I wrote a furious letter back stating that this was not a one way affair. If he wanted to see me he could just as easily come to Palestine. After all, boats and planes go both ways. In any case, I could not take leave for three months, I would lose my job! When I took it to the post office, I did not expect a reply.

My twenty-first birthday was fast approaching. As it happened I was owed holiday time for two weeks. I decided I would like to visit Cyprus. One or two friends, including Gaby, agreed to make up the party. I advised my boss that I was making the necessary arrangements and that I was looking forward to getting away.

'I am sorry, Harriett, my dear,' said Max from behind his desk. 'You will have to cancel.'

'But it's my birthday present to myself!'

'The whole office knows there is an important case pending.' He looked at me with solemn eyes. 'I need you here. You know that.'

I nodded miserably. '*The pig!*' I thought and stormed out.

When we learned of the trial date for the three Betar boys, I realised Max had been right all along. It fell at the time of my birthday. Instead of a holiday, I prepared to accompany him to the Jerusalem court room once more.

In my angst about my birthday arrangements I was completely caught up in my own affairs, so it came as a surprise when, a week before the trial, the boss did not appear in the office at his usual time. He never made an appointment that I did not know about. I suspected something was up as the telephone rang.

'Harriett, it's Millie Seligman here.' I held the telephone with one hand and opened the diary with the other, ready to pencil in any new appointment.

'Max is not well,' she said. 'He's not coming in. He is running a high fever. He tried to get out of bed, but his legs buckled under him.' She paused. 'He sounds delirious.'

It was awful news.

'If there is anything I can do,' I said, thinking, *'Thank Heavens I did not go away.'*

Over the next few days, Max's illness developed into pneumonia. We were increasingly worried about him. Even if he made a good recovery, which we all prayed for, he was unlikely to be able to plead on behalf of the three Betar boys.

With the help of my notes, a senior law member of staff collated the case for the defence as it had been developed by Max to this point. Then the papers were handed to a colleague in another firm who was requested to visit the boys in prison to get confirmation of facts, which he did. At the same time he obtained Powers of Attorney from them for him to proceed on their behalf instead of Mr Seligman.

At the time of the trial Mr. Seligman had not recovered sufficiently to attend. No matter how well the lawyers presented their case, the accused were without Max Seligman's pleading powers, his brilliant know-how and his natural charm in court.

News of the trial was quickly reported back to Jewish communities everywhere. As expected, all three were found guilty. One man, Zurabin, was given a long prison sentence. We could cope with that. As long as there was life, there was hope. But the other two, Ben Yosef and Schein-Amikam were sentenced to death.

Once more, we were aghast at the severity of the sentences. Special pleading began by everyone involved in the cause, just as they had done for Altman. This time we were confident we would succeed, because even though the intent had been to harm, no-one had actually been killed in the attack.

We soon heard that Schein-Amikam's sentence had been reduced to life imprisonment since he was under eighteen. However, the death sentence on twenty-five year old Shlomo ben Yosef stood. He was destined to be an example.

The Yishuv, the community of Jews in Palestine, was completely stunned. No amount of effort to save Ben Yosef was of any avail. There was no reaction from the authorities. No news leaked out until it was officially posted that he had been hanged by the British at Acre prison on 29th June, 1938. He was the first Jew to be sacrificed to the Mandate. It was said he went bravely to the gallows singing patriotic songs.

After the announcement of his death the whole community was distraught. Many religious Jews went into mourning for him and sat *shiva*, the seven days of mourning. In every synagogue, wherever there was a gathering of Jews, either in Palestine or anywhere in the world, the memorial prayer for the dead, Kaddish, was recited for Shlomo ben Yosef as if he were a personal member of the family. He had died for our cause and we mourned his passing intensely.

Chapter 15

Ramat Gan and Jerusalem (1938)

The office was deep in gloom after the execution of Shlomo Ben Yosef. Terrorism against us increased, inspired by the Nazi laws being enacted in Germany and Austria. It was a terrible 'cocktail' to swallow and we were out of patience with the British authorities.

In addition, my parents looked so worn out these days, working so hard, seeing nothing in return, that Esther and I talked about bringing them to Tel Aviv to live with us. But what would happen to the property? Perhaps we should encourage them to return to the States as my elder sisters suggested. Should we all go back? When I broached J.L. on the subject he was adamant to stay and farm.

'As our fathers planted for us, so I plant for my children,' he quoted from the Talmud.

'Papa, I don't understand you. You chose farming when I know you yearned to be an academic. You were always so learned, always reading. You are knowledgeable about so much - languages, astronomy, science. Yet you chose such a middle-class life, tied down with a large family.'

He raised his eyebrows. 'What should I have done? I married your mother. It was not her fault I gave her six children. I had to see that she and the children were all right.'

'You always provided for us, we were never in want,' I agreed. 'But at last when you can retire, you persist in staying here.'

'It is my dream,' he said resolutely.

I kept myself fit with early morning swims in the company of Haganah friends, all of whom had been in prison at one time or another, so I felt quite safe! Also, once a week after work I took lessons with Katya, a dancing teacher. As I was returning home one evening, still dressed in my playsuit and several streets from my apartment, a sports car drew up beside me, horn honking with Yona beaming at me from the driver's seat.

'Where have you been hiding?' he said.

'I've been busy. How about you?'

He looked his usual debonair self.

'Hop in, I'll give you a lift home and we can talk.'

I climbed in beside him and he revved the engine, turned the car around and drove the opposite way to Rothschild Boulevard.

'Hey, Yona! I have to get back. I'm going out tonight. I have to get dressed.'

'You look fine. I'm taking you to dinner.'

'I can't go dressed like this!'

'No problem. I'm taking you to my place.'

'Are you crazy? It's nearly dark. There's a curfew, for heavens sake. I don't want to be arrested. Take me home right now. Please!'

He pacified me. 'Don't worry. I'll get you home through a curfew. We'll just have a nice evening together. I've missed you.'

There was not much I could do. The car was speeding towards Ramat Gan. I may not have been a woman of the world, but I sure as hell knew what to do to him if he tried anything on, so I resigned myself.

His home in Ramat Gan was run by a housekeeper who politely welcomed me and served up a delicious meal. It was almost as if she had known I was coming.

'Harriett, will you marry me?' pleaded Yona after dinner. 'I can't get you out of my mind. I love you. It would break my heart if you refuse.'

'I could never marry a man my parents do not approve of,' I replied as always. 'You know that. Thank you for the food, even though you abducted me to eat it. Now please take me home.'

'Well, it is curfew time,' he warned.

I was getting angry.

'I know!' I shouted. 'And you had better make sure I get back safely and all in one piece!'

It was twilight as we walked out to the car.

'Don't worry,' he crooned. 'Get under the blanket on the back seat and stay quiet. One man on his own is not suspicious. We will easily get through the cordon.'

'We had better!'

I lay in the car feeling ridiculous. He had not driven more than a mile before the Palestine Police waved him down and peered into the back. Then someone lifted my rug and shone a torch into my eyes. How humiliating! The policemen seemed to find it amusing that the 'little lady' would have to return to the gentleman's home. No matter how much I protested we were turned back.

'This is a fine mess you've got me into!' I said furiously. 'I'm fed up and tired.'

I stormed into his apartment, opened his bedroom door and threw myself on to the bed, pulling the covers high over my head.

'At least let me lend you something to sleep in,' he offered.

There was no way I would undress in front of him.

'No thanks,' I mumbled, then sat upright and glared at him. 'I'll change first thing tomorrow, at home. And if you compromise me tonight I will kill you.'

He sheepishly sat down on the edge of the bed. We spent the night in the same bed, without talking and without touching.

Next morning, I could not bear to look at him and spoke in monosyllables. He drove me back to town with the dawn chorus. Outside my apartment, I jumped out of his car.

'Don't you ever do anything like that ever again or I will get the police on to you!' I yelled.

I slammed the door so hard that the car shook.

'Harriett, I will always love you!' he shouted as he drove off.

'Why aren't the men who love me, the men I love?' I asked myself as I stood under the shower letting the water clean off the night.

Two days later when I was recounting the kidnap to my friend, Phyllis, she laughed heartily.

'Haven't you heard?' she said. 'Yona got engaged yesterday.'

'So much for a broken heart and undying love,' I thought cynically.

*

Max Seligman was recuperating. I was still without the boss at work. I sat disconsolately at the typewriter with nothing to do and no one to write to. As expected, I had not heard from Maurice. I decided to cheer myself up by sending him a pseudo-legal document naming him as the respondent. The indictment was that he had stopped writing to me, the appellant. I refrained from naming a penalty.

To my relief he took the hint, swallowed his pride and wrote back a conciliatory letter by return. I poured out my despair in my reply to him.

'Everyone is lonely for everyone else, I don't know what to do. It makes me feel like I'm in a labyrinth which has only one entrance and fifty exits, but it is practically impossible to get out of any one of them.'

I stopped typing. I was certain he would not understand how I felt. He would simply return some homily about making the best of things, or try to persuade me to leave Palestine. I was just about to rip the sheet from the typewriter when the telephone rang.

'Is Mr. Seligman there?' The man had a South African accent, but I did not recognise the caller.

'No, he's not. Who's speaking please?'

'Mr. Kaye here.'

'May I help you?'

'Well, I would like to borrow a book.'

'If you tell me what book it is, I'll check if we have it in the office library.'

'It's *Salmon on Tort.*'

'Hold on.' I searched the shelves, then went back to the telephone.

'As it happens, I have found it. Of course, you may borrow it.'

'Thank you. I'll send round for it.'

I put the book to one side, did the paperwork for the borrowing and returned to my desk. The letter, half written, did express my feelings exactly so I typed on.

During the morning a suave well-dressed man entered the office. He was reasonably tall, with firm features on a clean-shaven face. His hair was dark and wavy. He was gorgeous! My mouth dropped open before I could recover myself.

'Miss Gold? I've come to collect *Salmon on Tort*.'

I recognised that accent but he was hardly a messenger boy. He was in his late twenties, very confident. I felt a frisson of excitement pulse through me like an electric current. I handed the book over but was too tongue-tied to say anything.

He smiled at me, saying, 'That is very kind of you. Goodbye!'

Then he was gone. I had absolutely no idea who he was. I had never come across him before.

'Wow! How do you ever find this man again?' I asked myself.

*

Rose improved our spirits by writing that she had decided to give up her teaching post for a few months to visit us in Palestine. She planned to be in Tel Aviv for Esther's marriage in the autumn. She was leaving the States on 2nd July and would arrive around 25th July. Then she would stay with us on an extended visit. My parents were delighted as we had not seen her for four years. If only all of us could be together.

Sol, with his humorous eyes and warm heart, returned to the small-holding for the summer. I loved my big brother very much. He quietly confided in me that he had had hair-raising experiences serving under Orde Wingate in the Special Night Squad. He did not specify what. He certainly looked worn out but smiled to himself when I remarked, 'The country has been much quieter lately.'

Esther made preparations for her wedding to Mattie. Neither of them had much money to speak of, but they were so in love that they radiated happiness. I supposed that was a good enough reason for marriage, which I believed was either for love or practical reasons. I was in no hurry to tie myself to any man and quoted Shaw's lines to her.

'Marriage is a rotten institution but there isn't a better one!'

'You are too much of a realist, Harriett,' said Esther. 'One day you will find yourself head over heels in love. Then you'll change your tune.'

'I am a realist,' I agreed, keeping quiet about the elusive stranger with the borrowed book on Tort. 'Just where are you and Mattie spending your honeymoon night?'

Esther looked sheepish. 'In your apartment?'

I sighed. 'I suppose I could stay with friends.'

'You are a great sister,' Esther hugged me.

I looked at my kid sister, now taller than I, with her beautiful face and happy, shining eyes.

'You will make a wonderful bride,' I said, hugging her back.

'How about inviting Maurice to my wedding?' ventured Esther.

'I'll think about it,' I said.

*

Rose arrived safely at the end of July. We spent time with our parents in Herzlia, happy to be reunited, tumbling over ourselves to exchange news. Plans for Esther's wedding, and in particular what we were going to wear, were the main topics of conversation. I was growing to be finicky about how I looked; my hair, my nails, my shoes, my suits. After all, smart clothes were part of a person's make-up and I always wanted to present a good appearance. These days bobby-socks were definitely out.

By August the climate in Palestine was very hot. The sun beat down on all unprotected areas, leaving the land dry and thirsty for water. In Herzlia, ripened crops on our small-holding were harvested in the early morning hours before they shrivelled in the heat. The deep blue Mediterranean stretched from the beaches away to the horizon, keeping silent about secret night landings.

Max Seligman had made a full recovery and suggested I take a few days off to show Rose the sights once he had made certain arrangements for our protection. We agreed we should visit the Holy city.

Jerusalem lay bathed in searing golden sunlight as Rose and I walked towards the Jaffa Gate, then through into the Jewish quarter.

'You know the story about the shoemaker's children without shoes?' I reminded Rose. 'I've been over here four years, but this is the first time I've really seen Jerusalem.'

'It has an aura all its own,' said Rose, smiling at our companion.

Earlier, Max had taken us to Police Headquarters where a British CID Officer, complete with a revolver strapped to his chest, was assigned to accompany us.

'Just to be on the safe side. Two lovely young women, walking around alone. And I know you, Harriett. You would throw caution to the winds in your enthusiasm.' Max had insisted.

While our escort walked a pace behind us, Rose and I made our way down the narrow street leading to the Wailing Wall. Several religious Jews were engrossed in prayer, their murmuring and singing rising in the clear air, their songs of praise echoing together with prayers for a better world. It filled my soul to see the huge stones that had been the wall of Solomon's Temple still evident after thousands of years. This was my city, my homeland, my Zion. It was with great emotion that Rose and I walked silently away.

Afterwards, we visited David's Citadel where an archaeological dig had unearthed coins and pottery over two thousand years old.

'Tangible history,' I said to our escort. 'Jerusalem was our capital long before America was discovered. Even before Europe was civilised.'

'I know,' he said. 'I cannot imagine what we British are doing here.'

Rosh Hashanah, the Jewish New Year, was special this year because Rose was with us. We spent Yom Kippur together and fasted quite easily, although the day always seemed to go so slowly. Mother and father were in the synagogue all day, but we joined them for the final part of the service to hear the Shofar blown. Afterwards we walked home together to break our fast.

Always a sense of peace and hopefulness pervades after the Day of Atonement, but this year people were worried about the future. There were rumours that the Jewish State was going to be much smaller than the Peel Commission had earlier specified, (only two thousand square miles - one-twentieth of the original figure). The area would be mostly coastline from Tel Aviv to Haifa. No good would come of it.

Impending disaster lingered a little way off whilst we celebrated Sukkot, the Harvest festival. Then came Simchat Torah when we celebrated reading the last and first chapters of the Torah. The first chapter started 'In the beginning...'. We prayed for a new start, a new era, a better future.

And all the while, we gave thanks that we had lived to celebrate these times. Jewish festivals in a Jewish homeland were what our dreams were all about.

CHAPTER 16
Tel Aviv (1938)

Maurice and I continued to write frequently to each other. We were both leading active, interesting lives and had much to tell each other. I tried to keep him up-to-date on the political situation as far as I could understand it.

I wrote, 'Max Seligman has been made acting Chairman of the Palestine Colony Association, which supports the idea that Palestine becomes a British Dominion as a viable alternative to partition.'

Maurice's reply was non-committal, except to say that he had been accepted as a candidate for Parliament. He had his own agenda.

I replied, 'You certainly have the power of speech it takes to fool the public into believing that you are the best fellow for the position.'

He had mentioned that his father was ill. One had to be practical.

'Don't let your business go for the sake of trying to get into parliament,' I added.

I really was not sure whether he was a dreamer or not. In England at any rate he was not facing our problems.

I continued. 'There are terrible things going on here although I am comparatively safe - except when I travel. One of my friends, Gaby, was ambushed and killed driving through Ramallah to Tel Aviv.'

Tears came at the thought of young, kindly Gaby, who had involved me in the charity work I enjoyed doing. His funeral had been attended by half of Tel Aviv.

During the summer there was an increase in riots and attacks on Jewish buses and settlements. A bomb exploded in Jaffa market, killing and wounding many Arabs. There was bloodshed on both sides which the British authorities attempted to curb with curfews and road searches. The newspapers were not allowed to print anything except official communiqués, which made things very unpleasant because we never knew just what was happening around us.

One Thursday evening we were working late in the office when we heard terrific shooting which did not stop for two hours. It sounded like a war going on. We could hear shots, machine guns and bombs going off. It was awful and only a mile or so away. None of us wanted to leave the building so we all held on until it quietened down and we felt it safe to go home.

Next day the official communiqué in the paper read:

'Last evening between 5:30 and 7:30 some shots were fired on the Jaffa-Tel Aviv border - the police inflicted casualties on the Band - number unknown.'

That was all we knew.

Underneath was a succinct cartoon showing a man being brought to hospital on a stretcher with the doctor asking *'Are you wounded?'* The man answers, *'I can't tell you - please wait for the official communiqué!'*

With the country the way it was, there were no affairs or parties of any kind whatsoever. I was grateful to spend some afternoons having lunch with Phyllis. I played with her baby daughter who laughed without restraint, taking everything as it came without trying to figure out life's problems. It was refreshing and relaxing to be with them. It took my mind off the outside world for a little while.

At the end of September Maurice wrote that he was relieved war in Europe had been averted. The British Prime

Minister, Neville Chamberlain, had just returned from Munich after his meeting with the German Chancellor. On the newsreels we watched as he waved a piece of paper declaring, 'Peace in our time.'

I was not so sure. Jews were being killed in Germany and Austria, and we thought that Britain had let us down. My feeling was that the Jews would have been much better if there had been a war.

Maurice suggested I return to London. How could I? I might consider going there for a holiday with Rose, but Esther's wedding was in November so there was little time. In any case my parents felt that he should come to Palestine to meet them first before I decided what to do.

J.L. was quite blunt with me.

'Unless you have some inkling whether you are interested in Maurice or not, do not think of going to London.'

My mother added, 'Harriett, if he is interested in you he should take three weeks to fly over and meet us. Then you can decide. We can make all arrangements here and then you can go back together.'

I did not know whether or not I agreed with them. I did not want to discuss it at length. I felt they were jumping to conclusions. But they insisted that it was Maurice's place to come and meet my family, so I wrote:

'*About us, you see I would like to go to London and it would even be quite alright to stay at your home - but my parents have very set ideas about some things and this is one of them. You could fly over here in two days. I would like to see you, but you may be disappointed in me. Because of all the events that have happened I have changed a lot in the past year. I really haven't the faintest idea of how we will react to each other - after all a year is a long time - not so much in*

154

your life - as you are more or less completely formed and your ways and ideas are quite set - but the past year has played havoc with me and I think I have changed quite a lot - not in looks at all - but inside somewhat. For me it is a meeting with an old and dear friend. If it should prove more than that - we shall see. My sister, Esther is having a quiet wedding in Tel Aviv. May I cordially invite you to come?'

*

On 3rd October, another Jew, Jacob Ben Moshe Kotek, aged 25 of Tel Aviv, was sentenced to death by the Jerusalem Military Court on a charge of carrying three automatic pistols, eight detonators, seven sticks of gelignite and two lengths of safety fuse. He was caught red-handed.

Once more Mr. Seligman was able to plead his defence successfully. The death sentence was commuted to life imprisonment.

At the same time twenty Jews were killed in cold blood by Arabs in Tiberias. Everything was fraught and unfair when you compared the harshness of Kotek's sentence while Arabs carried out such atrocities unpunished. I poured out my anger in my letter to Maurice.

On top of it all, everyone travelling in Palestine on any highway must now carry a pass - either single or permanent. It was going to be very difficult to arrange a pass for my parents simply to come to Tel Aviv for the wedding.

*

Esther's marriage ceremony took place on 3rd November, 1938. Friends and family gathered together in the pleasant gardens of our apartment in Rothschild Boulevard. Mother looked elegant in a calf-length, flower-embossed, black silk dress with red trimmings, a pretty artificial flower at her waist. J.L. wore his afternoon suit.

It was dusk when Esther, carrying a bouquet of orange blossom, came to stand beside her Matthew beneath the Chupa, the wedding canopy set under the stars. She looked radiant. Her thin white veil, held under a crown of orange blossom, floated over her long white dress. The four poles of the Chupa were decorated with flowers that scented the air in the cool evening. My parents, together with Mattie's mother and brother, stood either side of the bride and bridegroom as the Rabbi sang blessings over a goblet of wine. Then Mama held the goblet for Esther to take a sip after Mattie.

I held the bouquet for her as Mattie placed the wedding ring, as is the custom, on the index finger of Esther's right hand.

'Haray Aht Mekudeshet Li Betabat Zu Kedat Moshe Ve Yisrael' (*You are sanctified to me with this ring according to the law of Moses and Israel*).

The ring, not designed to fit that finger, only went as far as Esther's knuckle. When the Rabbi gave a little homily she slipped it onto the third finger of her left hand. Then Mattie broke a glass underfoot when everyone shouted 'Mazeltov!' before he lifted back the veil to kiss his beautiful bride.

They made a stunning couple. Tall, blond, good-looking Matthew and my elegant, slim, dark-haired sister, both charming and very much in love.

During the buffet reception, family reunions kept the atmosphere noisy and jolly. Everyone asked me the usual question: 'When will we dance at your wedding?'. I wanted to answer, 'When you get an invitation!'. But to be polite I simply replied, 'Eventually.'

At about nine-thirty, Rose and I, and a whole crowd of friends, made our excuses and slipped away to attend a charity

Tuberculosis Ball that evening. Almost the minute we arrived my dear friend Phyllis hurried over to me.

'Now listen, Harriett. I have someone who wants to meet you. His name is Eli, and I'm telling you I don't want any responsibility for introducing you. I won't have anything more to do with it.'

I laughed. 'Since when did I ever ask you to take responsibility?'

'Yes, I know.' She raised her eyebrows. 'But I'm just warning you!'

'Okay,' I said. 'I've been warned.'

My heart jumped as I recognised the gorgeous man she introduced to me. He obviously knew who I was. Hadn't I lent him *Salmon on Tort* all in a fluster? It was electric!

'Would you like to dance?' He guided me on to the floor.

He spoke beautifully as we danced and chatted. I soon found out he was a lawyer with his own office. He came from South Africa, his father was in business with Phyllis's father. All thoughts of Mac, Yona, Maurice or anyone else were dispelled as I floated around the floor in my white brocade with the Kelly green trim, looking my absolute best. Wasn't fate wonderful?

'Would you like to have dinner?' he said at last. He was older than I, very assured and, no doubt, experienced.

'Yes, that would be nice,' I replied casually. '*It would be wonderful*,' I thought.

'Well then, what day?'

Today was Thursday. Then there was the weekend in Herzlia to talk about the wedding. I must not seem too forward.

'Wednesday sounds okay to me.'

'Fine. You had better tell me where you live.'

'Rothschild Boulevard.' I gave him the full address.

'Would seven suit you?'

'Yes,' I breathed. 'Thank you.'

We danced on until the final waltz when we were about to part.

'Until Wednesday,' he said. 'I hope I remember your address!'

I was not about to repeat it. I threw back my head.

'If you don't remember my address that will be your tough luck!' I said.

'Touché!' he grinned.

I may have been younger and less experienced than he, but I sure was not going to let him get to me the way Mac had hurt me.

By seven on Wednesday I was looking good and ready to enjoy my evening with Eli. By seven fifteen he had not shown up.

'He has forgotten my address,' I said to Rose. 'If he's not here in five minutes, that's it. He's not going to mess with me. Women keep men waiting on the first date, not the other way around!'

At seven twenty-five I gave up on him and undressed.

At seven thirty Rose answered the door.

'I'm sorry, Harriett's gone to bed,' she said sweetly.

Eli was suitably taken aback.

'Would you just ask her to come and speak to me for a moment?'

She did. I appeared in my dressing gown looking vaguely astonished.

'I am terribly sorry,' he said.

'Well, you did say you hoped you would remember my address,' I countered. 'I assumed you had forgotten it.'

It was delightful teasing him. He was terribly sorry, he had not meant it. Would I please forgive him? Please wouldn't I join him for dinner? Please?

I managed to pretend to swallow my pride, got dressed and, winking at Rose, followed him to his car, a sparkling blue Mercury Ford - just *the* latest thing. He stopped outside a well-known restaurant, got out and waited for me to join him. I did not move. I watched as he came around and opened my door.

'Oh, I see we're used to footmen,' he said sarcastically.

'Oh no! We are actually used to gentlemen,' I countered.

*

The whole town was abuzz. Eli was quite a catch. We went out together regularly, but we were always having problems. He was very active in the Haganah and disappeared without notice at the drop of a hat. I understood. I knew if I did not hear from him he was off doing something important, which could happen any time.

On his return, he contacted me by telephone:

'Harriett, I'm back. I'm here. I'll pick you up at seven.'

I made a point of being there, ready for him even if he was late.

'I'm taking you to meet Alec, a great friend of mine from South Africa,' he announced one evening. 'He's just got engaged to a girl. I have not met her and he wants to know what I think.'

'Why would he care?' I was astonished.

'He trusts my judgement with women,' winked Eli.

'Oh, for heavens sake!' I exploded.

'Seriously though. He wants to meet you, and I want you to meet him. And then you can tell me what you think of her. All right?'

'You men always seem to need the approbation of your friends. I can't think why. I don't care if my friends like you or not!'

'You know they do like me,' he countered.

Alec and Eli shook hands heartily when they met. I was introduced to Zippora, a beautiful brunette, very slender with high cheek bones and a smiling face. She had been born in Latvia and spoke many languages. We dined out as a foursome at the San Remo hotel. Alec and Eli laughed and joked with each other throughout the meal, whilst Zippora and I found immediate rapport. By the end of the evening we had become great friends, promising to keep in touch no matter what. It was a good night out, Eli and I both approved of the match. They were obviously very much in love. I did not know if we were.

Eli's friends were mainly other South Africans. They were not part of the crowd at Arnold and Queenie's home, who were established Sabras in Palestine. I was therefore involved with two sets of friends who did not know each other.

Sometimes when Eli took me out to dinner his behaviour puzzled me. He would indicate to the waiter his favourite table and stride over to it without stopping.

'Why didn't you greet my friends?' I asked at the table, after everyone had hailed us on our entrance to the restaurant. 'I should like to introduce you. It is very rude to walk on past while I stop to say hello.'

'Just because they are your friends, does not mean they are mine,' he said scathingly.

'You are not very gentlemanly, are you?'

'I do not see the need to be everyone's friend.'

He had made his point. Also I appreciated that he was often very tired after days away in the mountains. Then we would spend a quiet evening in his flat simply having supper together. I was certain he wanted to marry me, but in his own time.

In the meantime, I was still corresponding with Maurice who had decided that he would definitely come to Palestine during the winter holidays.

'It will be wonderful to see you,' I wrote. 'But remember, I am not a cow to be looked over!'

'I can't wait to be with you again, Goldilocks' he replied, enclosing a studio photograph of himself. 'So that you remember who I am.'

Next day I had it framed and placed it on my writing desk in front of my apartment window. I was certain that when Eli called for me, he would be intrigued by the face of this strange man and want to question me about him.

'This is fun!' I thought, working out what I would say to Eli.

The photograph had not been on my desk for five minutes before Eli walked in. He bent to give me a kiss and noticed the picture.

'What the hell is Goodman doing on your desk?' he exclaimed.

I was so flabbergasted, I picked up the frame and threw it at him. How could I have imagined that I, born in the United States, and he born in South Africa, and Goodman born in London, all knew each other? I was mad. I had put it there so he would not have any idea who it was, to make him wonder what it was doing there and have to ask who was this friend of mine. A little jealousy perhaps might have done the trick.

'How do you know him?' I asked in amazement.

'That jerk! We were at Cambridge together!'

It turned out they hated each other. It was the wickedest twist of fate.

CHAPTER 17

Tel Aviv and Haifa (Autumn 1938)

Alec and Zippora were married at the house of the parents of my dear friend Phyllis, whom I had met on my first night in Palestine. Alec, also a South African, worked for Mr Braude, who had offered his elegant home in Tel Binyamin for the reception. It was the first wedding that Eli and I would attend together.

'Be careful!' warned Phyllis as we met in her parents' living room before the reception.

'Why should I be careful?'

'Everyone is looking out to see who is Eli's girlfriend.'

'That's half the fun,' I said. 'It's fine by me.'

'Don't take him for granted,' said Phyllis. 'He is not known for making people happy.'

'You keep warning me about him but don't worry. I can look after myself,' I replied.

Zippora appeared in her bridal gown looking radiant.

'Some men know how to treat a girl properly,' whispered Phyllis. 'I don't think Eli is one of them.'

Phyllis was really annoying me. I turned towards Zippora.

'You look a picture!' I exclaimed.

Zippora smiled serenely. She was one of those special kind of people who are loved by everyone. She was talented and artistic, utterly and completely charismatic. Every single person who met her would say she was their best friend.

'You are my dear friends,' she said, as we adjusted her veil and handed her the bouquet of orange blossom.

'Next year you and Eli,' she said squeezing my hand.

By the middle of November it started to rain; the first real downpour of the season. At the same time we heard the news about Kristallnacht, when Jewish property in Germany was smashed up and over two hundred synagogues destroyed. The heavens were angry in Palestine. Fierce lightning, thunder and strong winds whipped up the sea so that parts of Tel Aviv were flooded, even to the tops of cars in some places.

Esther and Mattie had gone to Herzlia for the week where mother happily fussed around them. I remained in Tel Aviv waiting to hear from Eli, but writing a long letter to Maurice saying that I hoped things in England had quietened down and people were living normally again since the scare of war had passed over. For our part, 'the country was more or less under military rule and things had been, thank heavens, a bit quieter.'

Maurice had not attended Esther's wedding. He had sent good wishes and a length of beautiful material for her to have made into an autumn coat with a velvet collar. When she showed it to me she was so excited.

'Oh, it's gorgeous! I must take a picture and send it to Maurice,' she exclaimed. It was as if he were already one of the family.

His letters to me became more intense. He wrote:

That faint American accent of yours still is music in my ears. Have you any idea how much and how often I have longed to be with you for just five minutes? Oh, I am sure you cannot be different now: more mature, no doubt, more serene and, probably, lovelier to look at than ever - but, essentially the same darling Goldilocks! And to think that in a matter of weeks I shall see you again!'

He had made up his mind. He was definitely coming to Palestine.

'Are you still typing letters to that jerk, Goodman?' asked Eli, looking over my shoulder as he picked me up from the office one afternoon.

'Sure, we are good pen friends,' I replied.

I did not dare tell him of the content of the letter or of Maurice's impending visit.

I was being kept busy in the legal office. Max Seligman's reputation was international and he corresponded with people in all parts of the world. One morning he handed me a letter.

'Will you type this for me?'

'But it's a French letter!' I exclaimed.

'Harriett, don't ever say that again,' he admonished.

'Well, it is. It's a French letter.' Was I stupid?

'No. It is a letter in French,' he replied.

I did not know what he was talking about until I mentioned it later to Eli, who took the trouble to explain it to me. I blushed. My fair skin always coloured up when I was embarrassed. The crowd would make fun of me. All they had to do was point at me and say, 'Look at her blush,' and I would go flame red all the way down to the tips of my toes. It was not a bit fashionable. In the olden days a girl blushed when she was ashamed, nowadays a girl was ashamed if she blushed!

*

Rose was due to return to the States early in December. Our plans to visit London together had been abandoned because of the political situation and our lack of finances. Her departure was going to leave me feeling very blue. I still missed my family in the States and hated the thought of our being continents apart. To cheer me up, she suggested we spend a couple of days in Haifa together before she embarked for home.

'I hate the train journey but I hesitate to go by road these days. Travelling is becoming so dangerous,' I said disconsolately.

Then I had an idea. 'If we want to avoid being shot on the road, let's go by plane.'

With my track record of travel sickness, I cannot imagine what made me propose such a journey. But intrepid as ever I telephoned my friend, Lee, who was the nephew of the founder of Rutenberg Electric Company, who were the original supplier of electricity to the country. I knew they had a small plane that often flew from Haifa to Tel Aviv and back, so I contacted him on my office telephone.

'Lee, it's Harriett.'

'Hello Harriett. What can I do for you?'

'Is the company plane going to be in town tomorrow?'

'Wait one moment. I'll let you know.' I could hear him rustling papers. 'Thursday, in Tel Aviv at eleven. Why?'

'Well, I have one big favour. My sister is sailing to the States at the end of this week. We just wanted some time together in Haifa, and I just thought....'

'You want a lift?'

'Yes, literally! Could we cadge one? Would there be room for the two of us?'

'Give me time to find out. I'll telephone you back.'

By the end of the day he had confirmed the flying arrangement. The plane would land and take off near the Yarkon River. Rose and I made our plans for an overnight stay in Haifa.

We left Tel Aviv at four in the afternoon, taking off into a dull sky. After we had been flying for ten minutes we came into a storm. It was black as blazes and suddenly I was not sitting in my seat but the plane seemed to be below me and I was left dangling in the air until suddenly, plop, I was back in my seat - and no sooner was I there than I found myself in mid-air again. I simply could not help being sick as a dog and I was never so happy to be down on solid ground again. Rose took me straight to our hotel, where I collapsed on the bed and slept deeply for a couple of hours.

'Feeling okay now?' Rose was sitting on her bed reading when I awoke.

'Much better,' I said. 'Ravenously hungry, in fact.'

'Aren't we going to your friend, Moses, for dinner tonight?' Rose reminded me. 'Hadn't we better get dressed?'

I rang to reception for a taxi. We arrived in the suburbs at eight o'clock, in time to enjoy a delicious dinner. Moses had just returned from Europe so we had an entertaining evening hearing of his travels, admiring souvenirs and looking at photographs. Before we knew it the time was ten-thirty, and curfew in Haifa was at eleven.

It was still raining cats and dogs as we left, trying to hail a taxi. Eventually one stopped and we asked him to take us to our hotel. Can you imagine, he did not know where it was? I could not remember the exact address or how to direct him, so he drove around asking numerous people the way. Finally we realised that curfew hour was upon us. We were furious with the driver as we now had to order him to return us to Moses. We were very angry and shouted at him as we left the cab, especially since he insisted we pay him for getting us nowhere.

Moses was the kindest host. He gave a bedroom to two bedraggled girls who were aching to sleep. When we awoke next morning we were treated to a delicious breakfast of fruit, cheese, yoghurt and cereals, washed down with good strong coffee.

'How are you spending the day?' asked Moses, as we tucked in.

'Shopping!' said Rose and I in unison.

'Well, afterwards I will meet you for lunch, then drive you around Haifa to show you the sights,' he offered.

When at five o'clock we were finally dropped at Haifa port we thanked Moses profusely.

'It has been a memorable last day for me,' said Rose. 'Thank you for being such a generous host.'

The liner, due to sail at nine, had only just arrived and was being manoeuvred into place. I wished to stay with Rose as long as possible. Who knew when we would be together again? I managed to pull some strings to obtain a pass to go on board with her when the time came.

In the meantime it was still raining. We hung about the quayside getting soaked and even more miserable at having to part. Eventually, we boarded and stayed together until eight, when it was time to hug farewell. Rose had been an absolute dear and I was sorry to say 'Goodbye'. We had gotten on so well.

What with the rain and my tears, I looked like a drowned rat by the time I arrived at my hotel. My feet were like two chunks of ice and I was so tired that I could hardly undress.

I returned to Tel Aviv next morning by train, continuing straight on home to Herzlia for Shabbat.

'Now that Rose has gone I'm so unhappy,' I said to Papa, expecting some sympathy.

He rounded on me.

'Don't talk happiness! I'll tell you what happiness is. It's being born healthy; growing up and marrying a healthy person; having healthy children - and your children bury you. That's happiness!'

I did not reply because I did not really understand what he meant.

A week after Rose's departure, my father's dream of running the farm in Herzlia was suddenly interrupted.

The telephone rang.

'Seligman & Levitsky's office,' I answered.

'This is the Hadassah Hospital. May we speak with Harriett Gold?'

'What's happened?' I went ice cold.

'I am afraid your father has had an accident. He has been brought in by ambulance.'

I gasped. 'Is he all right?'

'He has a broken leg. He says to tell your mother.' I relaxed, he was all right!

I managed to get a message through to Mama that J.L. was in hospital, and to reassure her. Then I left the office immediately and walked quickly to the Hadassah Hospital.

J.L. was sitting up in a hospital bed, obviously in pain.

'Darling, did you let Mama know?' were his first word.

'I could not tell her much. What happened?'

'I thought I would make an early start on the ploughing this morning. Suddenly I heard a shot, the horse reared and I fell into a rut. I tried to stand, but I couldn't. I called out but there was no one around. Eventually I managed to drag myself to the roadside.' He looked worn out with pain. 'Luckily for me my neighbour eventually found me and called the ambulance. So here I am.'

'Oh, Papa, what are we going to do with you? I wish you would give up farming and come to Tel Aviv.'

He shook his head adamantly.

'Not yet, my dear. I still have work to do. As the sages say: It is not for us to finish the task, but neither are we free to desist from it.'

There was no use arguing with him.

It was established that he had broken his thigh bone and would have to be in plaster up to his hip. I was terribly upset, it seemed so unfair. My father, so energetic and otherwise well, would not be able to walk about or work for months to come. He was to be confined to hospital for some weeks after the operation to set his leg. He would not take inactivity lightly.

'Do you know it is the first time in over thirty-five years that your father and I have not shared Shabbat together,' said Mama wistfully as she lit the Friday night candles in my apartment.

'You are the perfect couple,' I said, kissing her cheek. 'You never quarrel, do you? Sometimes I think you are too quiet.'

'Silence is something I tried, but your father got around me.' Mama chuckled. 'Years ago when I disagreed with him we had an enormous quarrel.'

'I don't remember one,' I said.

'Before you were born. So I didn't speak to him. I put his dinner in front of him and I stayed quiet all evening.' She laughed at the remembrance. 'And your father came home next day and said, 'How are you?' And I still stayed quiet. So he said, 'How are our children?' and I didn't answer.'

'He always asks 'How are the children?'' I said.

My mother's eyes smiled.

'He said, 'Listen my dear, if I ask you how you are and you don't want to answer, that's your business - but when I ask you how are *our* children you have no right not to answer – they are my children too.'

She began to laugh. 'He had such a funny expression on his face that we were both laughing with each other.'

By this time my mother was wiping her eyes.

'He always got round me after that, even when you were grown up, by teasing me *So how are the children?*'

'And there was I believing that he really wanted to know!' I said, finally initiated into their private joke.

If only I had someone to share an intimate life with. I felt inundated with problems. I wanted so much for Eli to marry me, it would solve most of them. I could stay near my parents in Palestine, have children and build a family home in Zion. That was what I had been brought up for wasn't it? This was my father's dream, and now it had become mine.

When Chanukah came around, Esther, Mattie, Sol and I gathered at home in Herzlia to cheer up Mama. We felt sorry for father, but even more for ourselves.

'It will be the first time in all our married years that your father has not lit the Chanukah candles,' repeated our mother pensively.

On top of that, Esther, after feeling unwell several days later, was suddenly doubled up with stomach cramps and in terrible pain. Mattie was beside himself when he called the doctor. Stomach poisoning was diagnosed and she had to have her stomach pumped. She was very weak afterwards. We insisted she stay in bed for a week to get rested. Gradually she began to get her colour back and feel better.

I realised how much I had taken for granted, and how J.L's prophecy of happiness was true. We had all been so very healthy that we had found other things to complain about. Now I understood that no matter what other circumstances arose, if you were healthy you could overcome everything.

CHAPTER 18

Tel Aviv (1938 – 1939)

In the last week of December Maurice booked into the San Remo hotel in Tel Aviv. I was sick with apprehension at seeing him again. I had never mentioned Maurice to the crowd. The only person besides my family that I confided in was my best friend, Phyllis, whose husband had also been at Cambridge with both Maurice and Eli.

'You'll have to keep them apart,' Phyllis said practically.

I agreed. I hurried round to Esther's apartment and implored her and Mattie to keep Maurice busy so that I could still have an occasional date with Eli.

'That won't be easy,' she said.

After work I left to meet Maurice, the man who seemed madly in love with me. The man in whom I had confided my thoughts in so many letters since we had first met eighteen months ago.

It was an awkward meeting. Maurice, as good-looking and elegant as ever, came eagerly towards me as I entered the foyer and attempted to embrace me like a lover, but I somehow pulled back. At that instant he knew I was not *his Goldilocks*. For all the deep conversations we had held on paper, we made polite talk over dinner until it dawned on me that he had come over to ask me to marry him, or at least extract a promise that I would follow him to London soon.

'You're the girl I want,' Maurice announced after dinner, when I had recovered my composure. 'You know I have always loved you ever since we first met, and although I know these things are uncontrollable, I do so much want you to love me too, darling.'

I drew in my breath, he was so persuasive.

'One thing I do know, Harriett, is that I could make you very happy because, well I just feel it.'

How could he know I was torn in two? I shook my head. I was so emotionally upset at the thought of having to make a decision between him and Eli, that next day I feigned illness so I would not have to see him at all. It was making me physically unwell. I turned to my parents, perhaps they would settle the matter as they had with Yona.

By now, J.L., with his leg well plastered up to his thigh, was convalescing in Herzlia, with mother tenderly looking after him. I arranged to take Maurice to meet them at the weekend. He was pleased to have the chance to win them over. His cultured English accent and impeccable manners indicated he was a gentleman, obviously well educated and financially well off. On top of that, he was knowledgeable about Judaism and appeared very devout. My parents liked him very much, but sensed my predicament.

'What's the hurry to get married?' said my mother wisely.

'Mama is right. I cannot accept your offer, not straight away,' I said.

'Perhaps my persistence will win you over on New Year's Eve,' said Maurice when we parted on Sunday evening in Tel Aviv. I gasped. I had forgotten I was due to attend a ball with Eli.

'I do like you. I do care for you Maurice, but...' I trailed off in despair. I simply could not tell him about Eli, or even about my dismay at having to leave my family again. I still missed my older sisters and if I settled in England I would lose Esther and Sol as well as my parents. It was something I hated to think about.

172

'It's all right, Harriett,' Maurice said gently. 'Take your time.'

He bent and kissed me lightly before walking away to his hotel.

On Monday morning the office telephone rang.

'Hello Harriett, it's Molly.' She was one of Eli's crowd of friends. 'Just who were you with last week?'

'Nobody.'

'Are you kidding! You were seen with an Englishman. Is he one of the British mandated hierarchy?' She paused for my reply but I kept quiet. 'He's obviously not Jewish. What's going on?'

'Nothing.'

'Are you in trouble?'

'I'm not, Molly. Trust me.'

'I know you work for Max Seligman. Are you working behind the scenes for him?' She certainly was persistent.

'I'm busy. Please don't bother me, I can't talk about it. You understand, don't you?'

'Just take care of yourself,' she warned.

*

Esther helped me out on New Year's Eve. She turned up at the San Remo hotel to make my excuses to Maurice.

'Harriett cannot see you tonight. She is not well, she doesn't look well either!' she explained.

She was right. I was in turmoil.

Maurice, ever the tactful Englishman, said he understood. He spent the last evening of 1938 having dinner at the hotel with Esther and Mattie.

In the meantime, Eli arrived at my apartment expecting to escort me to the New Year's Eve ball with Alec and Zippora. By now even he could see I was not looking my best.

173

'Don't let's go out,' I pleaded. 'Let's stay at home at your flat. I don't feel up to partying. Can we see in 1939 quietly together?' That way I could not possibly bump into Maurice out on the town.

'That's fine by me,' agreed Eli.

When midnight struck, Eli and I stood opposite each other, raised our glasses of champagne and toasted 'To the future!'

But was it going to be our future together?

Early in the office on 1st January 1939, I answered the telephone brightly.

'Harriett? How do you feel? You are obviously feeling better!' It was Maurice. He could not wait!

'Well, everyone gets better!' I retorted angrily. 'I could be dying but I always get to work.' I realised I was being perfectly horrible, so I calmed down. 'Now I feel well, I look forward to seeing you tonight.'

'*Thank God,*' he whispered.

Maurice was waiting for me in the foyer of his hotel. He came forward expectantly, took hold of my hand and led me through the bar into the crowded restaurant. I was in such a daze that, although I could hear acquaintances greeting me, I could only respond with a weak smile whilst Maurice beamed and waved hello.

As he held the chair for me to sit down, he bent close and whispered a kiss on my cheek.

'Maurice, please.'

'You look pale. Let me order. Then we can talk.'

'It seems easier to write to you than talk to you.'

'I know. We are so close in our letters. When you write *'Maurice darling'* my heart leaps. I have yearned to be with you, you know that.'

Over dinner he urged, 'Harriett, marry me!'

I looked around the restaurant where my friends sat talking and laughing. I was in my own milieu, amongst my people. I did like Maurice. I enjoyed his company, but was that enough? I felt it was no longer fair to string him along.

'I am truly sorry,' I said, turning the cutlery in my hand. 'I thought my feelings were other than they are. Please Maurice, don't keep pressing me to decide. I love it here. I don't want to leave Palestine.'

'I understand completely how you feel,' said Maurice. 'Believe me, you would be just as happy in London. My parents would love you as much as I do. But take your time. I am prepared to wait.'

I sighed. He was so persistent. My only defence was to be cool and collected, which I was finding very hard to do.

In her apartment next day, Phyllis was concerned for me.

'You look awful,' she said when I arrived for lunch. 'How's the Eli versus Maurice situation?'

'I am in turmoil,' I said. 'I know I have to marry one of them - or get rid of them both. I just don't know what to do. It's making me physically ill. I can't cope with the situation at all.'

'They are both very desirable men,' said Phyllis. 'But are you really in love with either of them?'

I shook my head. 'I don't know!'

'I think you're just in love with love,' said Phyllis crisply.

*

The eight days spent in Palestine were a bitter disappointment to Maurice and a trial for me. He tried to repair our relationship, while several times I made excuses so I could see Eli without Maurice knowing, and vice versa. It was the first time I regretted having more than one boyfriend.

175

On the last evening of his stay, Maurice once more asked me to marry him.

'No, I can't,' I repeated. 'My parents are here. It would be too great a wrench.'

He looked dejected.

'I don't want to extend this agony for both of us,' I said emphatically. 'I don't want to leave Palestine. I don't want to marry abroad, and I don't want to give you hope where there is none.'

Maurice pursed his lips, then smiled.

'I'd rather be hopeful,' he said.

'No. It's finished,' I said categorically, then retracted. 'Let's stay friends. Let's not write so many letters to each other. Leave space between us. I will contact you, but not yet. Give me time to recover from whatever is making me unwell. I just want to be alone.'

He was ashen.

I continued. 'I am truly sorry. I can't explain it. It is nothing you said or did. It is just fate.'

'Harriett, don't do this to me! I leave tomorrow. Won't you come to Haifa with me to see me off?'

'I rather feel it would be putting salt on a festering wound if I did. I have enjoyed being with you and having you here. It has only made me unhappy to feel I made you unhappy.' I trailed off. Then for some reason I added, 'But don't give up on me. I will give you a definite answer by April.'

That would give me time to establish Eli's intentions and, more importantly, delay the decision to leave Palestine. When we said goodbye to each other that night, I did not think I would ever see Maurice again.

Maurice wrote a farewell letter, delivered early next morning, saying how difficult it had been for him in a new country with new people, different food and so on and blaming himself for what had occurred. It nagged for a reply before he left in a few hours time. I knew full well that other circumstances had made it impossible for me to know how I really felt about him. I scribbled a reply full of excuses of tiredness and of being unsettled by his visit. I sent best wishes to him and his family and signed my note 'Most sincerely'. I made sure it would be in his hands before his departure for England. I did not say it was a guilty conscience as much as anything that had made me so horrible to him. I went back to bed, turned my head into the pillow and sobbed.

Mattie and Esther rounded on me when they returned from Haifa after accompanying my English suitor to the port.

'You made the man very upset and disgruntled,' said Mattie.

'The way you treated him, I'm not surprised,' said Esther.

But she was in two minds as well because, despite liking Maurice very much, she did not want me to leave Palestine either.

The whole situation had left me so emotionally exhausted that I kept to my bed for two whole days afterwards and, for the only time in my life, felt happy to be ill.

CHAPTER 19

Hanita and Tel Aviv (1939)

The minute Maurice left for London the strangest thing
happened to me. I missed him. That is, I missed 'talking'
to him. I know I had insisted we delay corresponding for a
while, but I had the uncontrollable urge to write to him. I was
still in bed and just about to put pen to paper when Sol turned
up in my apartment.

'Hi, Harriett. You look terrible!'

'I'm fine really. Just too much partying, you know.'

He sat on my bed.

'The family is concerned about you. Now listen, I'm
heading for Hanita tomorrow. Tell your boss you won't be in
for a few more days and come with me on a little tour.'

'I don't know,' I replied lamely, but he insisted that a
change would do me good. I felt too washed out to argue so
eventually I agreed.

'I'll pick you up first thing,' he said, getting up to leave.

'Not too early,' I pleaded.

He ruffled my hair affectionately.

'Pack warm clothes and a blanket,' he added as he closed
the door. *What had I let myself in for?*

Next morning we boarded the train from Tel Aviv to
Haifa. On arrival we went to the bus terminal and waited for
the single decker to leave for Safed. The rattling bus climbed
up towards this biblical town, ancient seat of Jewish learning.
Sol and I walked together through narrow streets where
bearded scholars and pupils wearing sideburns and kipot, the
small cap covering the head, met together to read and

interpret the Torah, which is the first five books of the Old Testament. There was a strange, peaceful quietness about the place. So much so that before I knew it I was scribbling a note to London saying, 'Maurice Darling, I am in Safed with my brother...'

We made our way to the rendezvous point where a lorry with a smiling young driver, Ben, was waiting to take us even higher to Hanita. It was still wintery, wet and cold. We bumped along rocky tracks until we saw the watchtower looming ahead. The truck skidded through the stockade fence, past several tents and stopped outside a large wooden building. Ben beeped his horn and a dozen or so chalutzim (young men and women pioneers) clambered on the back to unload provisions and come around to shake my hand and embrace Sol.

'Sol was here last year when we were sent to these upper Galilee hills to start this settlement,' Ben explained. 'Haganah members guarded us whilst we staked out the land and built the perimeter stockades. There was no road then, so we all had to carry up equipment on our backs like mules.' He grinned. 'This is quite an improvement, isn't it?'

'You are still clearing the land,' I observed as a group of chalutzim were straining to drag away a huge boulder with ropes. Smaller boulders were lifted by hand and added to the stockade.

'We have cultivated a patch back there near one of the first houses. We've put in onions, potatoes and some tomatoes. We have to clear each piece of land by hand, then dig it over for the first crops to be planted in over two thousand years or more.' He paused with the enormity of this reality. 'We have to do it in stages. When the first house was built everyone moved in until the next house was ready. We don't have all the modern conveniences yet. If you want one it's over there.' He pointed to a rickety wattle frame hut in the distance. I grimaced inwardly.

'Harriett!' exclaimed a girl who came running towards me.

'Babra, I didn't know you were here! Last time I saw you was in Herzlia. I knew you were an idealist. So this is what you are up to.'

Come on in,' she invited, edging me into their sparse living area. 'We have another special visitor today. Our security officer Yitzak Sadeh is sending up Lieutenant Moshe Dayan for a briefing. I'll introduce you later. Come, eat and drink.'

That night I lay down to sleep on the wooden floor, fully dressed and wrapped in a blanket. When dawn came and I needed the loo, I found myself up to my knees in mud trudging towards the privy, which was just a hole in the ground.

'Return to us next year, you will see a difference,' they said as we made our goodbyes. 'We are starting a settlement at Dafna soon, then more. We need our own land and we are prepared to work for it.'

I was filled with admiration. These settlers were prepared to battle the land and the elements, with little money and no luxury, to gain a foothold in a Jewish State. I knew I did not have their strength of character. No way could I endure such physical deprivation.

Sol was his usual cheerful self when he delivered me safely back to Tel Aviv. 'I thought it would do you good to see how faith moves mountains,' he said.

And I agreed.

A letter from Maurice awaited me saying he was back and found London as nice as ever. Nothing of his impressions of Palestine. He still persisted in trying to persuade me to go to

England. I wrote back explaining my concerns about my parents, about Sol, about Esther, and the whole Palestine situation.

'I am not so much busy as bothered. About ourselves, it is very difficult for me to make up my mind with so many outside influences in my life. I think of you often, but there are too many ties which absolutely keep me from saying anything definite.'

There were ever widening differences between the Arab and Jewish communities. In February 1939 the British convened a conference in London to mediate between the two sides who refused to meet each other, let alone talk. The Arab Higher Committee wanted to stop Jewish immigration and all land transfer to Jews. They wanted an end to the Palestine Mandate, and for it to be replaced by an independent Arab Palestine linked to Britain by treaty.

On the other hand, the Yishuv, the Jewish community in Palestine, headed by the Zionist leaders in London, Dr. Chaim Weizmann and David Ben-Gurion, demanded the fulfilment of the 1917 Balfour Declaration, which was an entitlement to have a Jewish National home. Jews should have the right to buy land freely and they demanded unrestricted immigration. In view of the rise of Nazism, the Zionists knew this was an immediate necessity.

Britain was caught by the ever-looming prospect of war with Germany and tried to placate both sides. As a result, in May 1939, a White Paper was published limiting Jewish immigration in Palestine to a total of only 75,000 over five years, even from Nazi Germany. The Haganah was to be disbanded. We were devastated and despondent.

Overcrowded boats were sent secretly to Palestine carrying desperate Jewish refugees attempting to reach safety, only to be imprisoned and deported by the British authorities. There seemed no escape anywhere in the world from the murderous intentions of the Third Reich.

The luxury liner 'St. Louis' sailed from Hamburg to Cuba, holding 930 Jewish refugees, all with entry visas to Cuba. It was refused entry in Havana and also in the United States. The ship was forced to return across the Atlantic and disembark in Europe.

What could we do? Many young people marched through the streets, with flags flying to demonstrate their feelings.

Amongst my friends, Eli voiced his anger over the White Paper. He was astute enough to know that there was going to be a fight with the British. In my company, over a drink with Alec and Zippora, he berated the British for their short-sightedness and intransigence, even though as a South African he held a British passport.

Maurice also sent me a long letter about the political situation which he knew a great deal about, but which was one of my weakest subjects. I could not fathom it, or see a way out of our problems.

I replied: 'Things in general, look bad - and as we have done in the past we must go on in the future hoping.'

I did not mention my dilemma with Eli.

*

By March the social season started again. During Purim I went to a couple of affairs, but the spirit was missing.

'Not only is the political situation such as to dull one's spirits, the weather lets forth such storms as to make one afraid to go out of doors,' I wrote. It mirrored our horror at what was going on in Germany. The situation could not get any worse. It must get better.

Arnold and Queenie still entertained the Palestinian born friends I had become so fond of. We did our best to keep up our spirits against the background of oppression in Europe. News was filtering through from Poland of Jews being humiliated, beaten and murdered by the invaders. If only we could get them out.

My other group of friends, immigrant South Africans of whom Eli was one, despaired of the British sanction on Jewish immigrants. Dr. Chaim Weizmann's statement to the Commission that there were 'Six million Jews for whom the world is divided into two parts: places where they are not allowed to live and places they cannot enter,' resonated with awful truth. J.L.'s dream of a Jewish homeland offering safety and shelter to a stateless and persecuted people was farther away from reality than ever.

I often visited Zippora in her artist's studio where she painted professionally. She was talented, multi-lingual, intelligent and full of vitality. She was very happily married to Alec and contented to live in Palestine, where all her family were safely settled.

'Even though I have the most important part of my family here, I still miss my elder sisters, and the wonderful extended family in the States who were such fun to be with,' I confided.

'You will create your own family over here,' she assured me. 'You too will be happily settled. You are such a clever, practical person, Harriett. I do admire you.'

I laughed. 'But I admire you! I don't have your creative ability.' I paused in self-assessment. 'But I suppose I have other good points. I am great at organising people, and I'm a good judge of character.'

Zippora laughed. 'That's why we get along so well We are a mutual admiration society!'

Esther and I were spending more time together since Mattie's work had been transferred to Jerusalem. We planned to go up to Jerusalem to look for an apartment after the festive season.

At the start of Passover we gathered in Herzlia for Seder night. I had already helped Mama clean the kitchen thoroughly and clear all chametz (leavened bread and non-Passover foods) from the house. We set the table with Matza and wine. Then we filled the Seder plate with parsley, a burnt egg, a shank bone, marrar (bitter herbs), charoseth (apples, nuts, cinnamon and wine ground together) and salt water. All these were symbols of the story of our deliverance from Egyptian slavery when Moses asked Pharaoh to 'Let my people go!' That it was the turning point in Israel's history when we became a new nation, born to live in freedom and independence in the Holy Land, made the festival all the more poignant in these modern times.

Papa and Sol read the Hagaddah, which was the story of our flight from ancient Egypt. We sat around the table, leaning as free men, eating and drinking the prescribed four small glasses of wine. When we lifted the final glass and toasted '*Next year in Jerusalem!*' it seemed a good time to approach an old subject.

'Papa, why don't you and Mama sell the farm and go to Jerusalem?' I ventured. 'Mattie and Esther will be there and you ought to be quite happy living in the Holy City. It would be an easier life for you both.'

'We shall see!' said J.L, against our encouragement. 'Be patient all of you.' I felt doubtful that he would agree.

On my return to Tel Aviv a parcel had arrived from London enclosing half a dozen Irish linen handkerchiefs, beautifully embroidered and wrapped. They were Maurice and exactly what I would have chosen myself. He certainly had good taste. When I wrote to thank him he was treated to a twelve page hand-written letter full of gossip.

'Speaking of wallowing in bed, believe me I'm darned lucky I had that rest. I'm making up for it tenfold. I haven't been so busy in months - but it is pleasant - and now I've had a perfectly gorgeous bath, done my hair, washed and ironed and had a general spring cleaning, I want to write to you.'

I did feel better, so I added *'Dearest Maurice'* and finished *'Do write, regards to all, Love Harriett.'* That should keep him happy.

*

Ever since my mother's outings to Shartenburg's store in New Haven, springtime was always the season to buy a new dress. It naturally cheered me up to go shopping. There were new season's clothes in my regular dress shop.

'This is just your kind of dress,' said the sales lady, finally convincing me that I looked stunning in a rather austere navy linen.

'It's far too large,' I said, turning to the mirror.

'We can alter it for you by next week,' insisted the sales lady.

'I don't have any money to leave as deposit,' I ventured, hoping she would negate the sale.

'We know you as a good customer, madam. Please don't worry about it.'

So against my better judgement I agreed to take it on 'tick'. But I just knew it was not right for me, and worried about it for days before I had the courage to return to the shop.

'Look, I realise I have left no deposit on that dress, but honestly I would never wear it. I appreciate it has been altered to fit me, but - ' I hesitated before I blurted out, 'Would you accept ten shillings and finish the matter?'

I expected the shop to be furious, but they were very nice about it.

'Would you like to choose another instead?' offered the sales lady. 'We should not like you to be unhappy.'

'Fine!' I radiated relief.

The shop assistant ran through the rails searching for another garment more to my liking and held out a highly coloured, pure silk dress which, when I tried it on, fitted me perfectly.

'That's so smart!' I exclaimed. 'I must have it.'

So the transaction was made, at double the cost of the first dress.

'What the hell!' I thought. 'Eli will appreciate it, and I love looking good next to him in public.'

Eli and I appeared together more often than not. I was forever being chivvied 'When are we going to dance at your wedding?' I wondered about that myself, but he seemed in no hurry. However, he was always calling around to talk, or take me out to eat, or over to his place for company. He was very busy, both in the office and with the Haganah, and was often too tired to do anything more than lounge in his chair and doze off. I was prepared to wait.

My father recovered slowly from his accident. He came to Tel Aviv to attend a hospital appointment for the plaster to be removed. At last he could walk aided by crutches.

J.L. visited me before returning by car to Herzlia. At that time Eli was in my apartment and I could hear the two men chatting whilst I made tea in the kitchen. I had not said a word about wanting to get married, but I realised my father was shrewd enough to understand the situation and was sizing Eli up.

When it was time to leave Papa struggled to stand with his crutches, pursing his lips, unused to moving without the plaster.

'Let me help you.' Eli started up towards him and put his hand under my father's arm.

'I can do it myself, thank you.' J.L. gave him the most withering look as Eli took a step back.

Beside the taxi, J.L. turned to me.

'You cannot possibly marry that man,' he said.

I had always admired my father as a sound judge of character, but this time the accident must have clouded his judgement.

'Papa!' I protested.

'He is a very nice, intelligent man, but he has no brains. If he doesn't appreciate a disabled man doesn't want help unless he asks for it, he doesn't understand anything! He made me seem like an invalid. He is insensitive. Harriett, he is not the man for you.'

This was one time I knew my father was wrong.

The next day Eli phoned to say he would pick me up as usual. I wore my new silk dress, just designed to be taken out to dinner in. When he arrived he had not even changed, he was still in his shorts. He took a double look at me.

'You look so beautiful tonight,' he said. 'I would like to show you to the whole world.'

'What's stopping you?' I countered.

He smiled wryly. 'Do you mind if we get something to take back to my place? I can't face going out tonight.'

'Okay.' I shrugged away my disappointment.

Next morning the office telephone rang.

'Harriett, it's Molly. Where were you last night?'

'I was with Eli. We were having supper. He came back late.'

'Why weren't you at the Gat Ramon Hotel?'

'Why should I have been at the Gat Ramon?'

'Because we all waited for you both, with Alec and Zippora. Eli's father was here to meet you. We all expected you to come to dinner. We did not eat until nine o'clock!'

'That's the first I've heard about it,' I said putting the receiver down, slowly realising the truth.

I had never been introduced to Eli's father. Last night, Eli had obviously backed out from showing me to his family. He did not want to marry me. I felt sick with anger at his deception. How could J.L. have been so right?

I was twenty-one. There was a man the other side of the world who did want me. Okay, I had only been with him for four weeks, two in London, two in Palestine, but I felt I knew him from all the letters we had exchanged. My parents liked and approved of him. It seemed that fate was making the decision for me. I was going to have to leave Palestine.

I went home and wrote to Maurice saying, 'I told you I would give you my answer by the end of April and 'yes' I will come to London and I will marry you!'

CHAPTER 20

Tel Aviv and Haifa (Summer 1939)

My relationship with Eli rapidly cooled. When I next saw him I could hardly look him in the face. He never explained why he had not introduced me to his family, and I was too hurt to ask. He seemed quite unaware of how wounded I felt.

One evening when he called at my apartment I plucked up the courage to mention Maurice. When I told him of my plans he exploded.

'You are never going to marry that idiot!'

I refrained from retorting that it was plain he did not want to marry me.

'I love London,' I answered. 'I love the culture and the people. I am certain I will be happy there.'

He left my apartment, slamming the door. Well it was his loss I told myself, picking up my pride and deciding to throw myself into charity work and the office.

The hot news was that Harriett Gold was going to marry the mysterious English man who had appeared in the San Remo hotel at the start of the year. My acquaintances were aghast.

'You can't be thinking of leaving us,' said Molly, who had set her heart on my marrying Eli.

Zippora was more conciliatory.

'It is good to start a new life with the man you love,' she said, giving me a kiss of congratulation.

'I am giving myself three months to leave my job and sort myself out,' I told her.

Phyllis too was upset because she and I were dear friends who loved each other's company. Over the years, since we had met on my first day in Palestine, we had lunched together once or twice every week. She was married now to Yadim, the son of a judge, and had a baby. She was my confidante and knew me perhaps better than anyone. I should miss her immensely.

'I can't believe you are going to England,' she said. 'Are you certain you are doing the right thing?'

I was not, but fate seemed to be edging me that way. Something inside me seemed to be insisting it was the correct decision. Maurice cabled that he was overjoyed and assured me I would never regret it. He was putting arrangements in place to make me his wife as soon as possible. August would not come soon enough for him.

In the meantime, I wrote to my sisters in the States informing them of my decision and inviting them to London. My parents were phlegmatic about the whole thing.

'We must organize your trousseau,' said my mother.

She arranged to meet me at the dressmakers where we spent ages choosing materials for new outfits and a wedding dress design. I was swept along by the excitement of it all.

Every one who knew me well was genuinely happy for me, except for Max Seligman who seemed rather put out.

'I won't leave until the last minute,' I assured him.

'You won't leave until you have replaced yourself and trained up the replacement,' he insisted.

He was preparing for yet another court case in Jerusalem.

Every day was edging me towards the inexorable parting from my family and Palestine. I tried not to think about it. Leah wrote that she was happy to go to England to arrange the wedding reception. She intended to be waiting there when I arrived. Everything seemed to be falling into place.

Early in June two gentlemen appeared in the office requesting to see Mr. Seligman.

'Do you have an appointment?' I asked, knowing that Max was gathering his papers together to go on a trip to Europe next day.

'We do not need one. We are policemen,' said one, showing his credentials.

'Wait one moment please.' I knocked on the boss's door and entered.

'Mr. Seligman, the police are outside.' I must have looked startled.

He rose from his seat.

'That's all right, Harriett. I have been expecting them. Show them in.'

I thought no more about it until I heard later in the day that Max had been served with a subpoena, with twenty-two counts alleging conspiracy to organize illegal immigration into Palestine. It was preposterous. No one was more upright than Max Seligman, and although his sympathies for persecuted and stateless Jews were well known, it was unthinkable that he would conspire against the British government and break the law. It was obviously a trumped up charge by the authorities to 'get Seligman if at all possible'. He had been far too successful in defending such cases.

The office was in turmoil. The boss's plans for visiting England were shelved immediately since he had to appear in court the following Tuesday. We had complete faith in his ability to plead his cause.

He decided not to conduct his own defence. The venue of the trial was to be Jerusalem. The Attorney General considered that the court in Tel Aviv would be too friendly. After all, Max was very well known and appeared there regularly on behalf of clients, invariably earning them lighter sentences.

A registered letter from Maurice arrived the week of the trial. He apologized for missing the date of my birthday, but hoped we would be together for next year onwards. He had also heard about the Seligman case from the newspapers and promised to follow it carefully. Max had his full support.

'Everyone I know in England appears to be appalled by the government resorting to these trumped-up charges,' he wrote.

The hearing against Max Seligman was on 27th June. Max had insisted I stay to run the office during his absence. Naturally Millie Seligman was by her husband's side in Jerusalem. It was reported that the courthouse was packed, but I had to wait in Tel Aviv on tenterhooks for the outcome.

The case was evidently biased against him. Friendly witnesses were prevented from appearing because of the curfew between Tel Aviv and Jerusalem. During a severe cross-examination Max calmly expressed the view that every Jew had a right to come to Palestine; otherwise the term 'Jewish National Home' had no meaning. That was his belief, but he was not a member of any organization helping illegal immigrants. Witness for the prosecution, a Major Gilpin, was patently lying when he said Seligman had bribed guards to turn a blind eye to the illegal landings. I knew Max would never bribe anyone, he was too much of an upright Englishman.

There were two judges, one British, who evidently had orders from above to charge Max.. The other, an Arab judge, had wanted to acquit him. He confided later that he would lose his job if he did not agree.

The trial was well reported and we felt it would be a travesty of justice if the judges brought in a guilty verdict.

However, although sixteen counts were dismissed, Max Seligman was found guilty on three charges of conspiracy to assist Jews to enter Palestine illegally. He was sentenced to a period of six months imprisonment.

Max was given bail and the Yishuv held its breath for the outcome. Everyone expected that it would take months for his appeal to be heard, but the British were intent in their purpose. Against all normal procedure, the appeal was rushed forward for the coming week. It was heard on 7th July. The Court of Appeal announced it would not interfere with the sentence of guilty, but directed a reduced sentence from six months to four. Also Max should be given 'special treatment' whilst in prison. He would be permitted to wear his own clothes, not have to do prison work, have food sent in and sleep on a bed instead of the floor. In any event, to a man of Max Seligman's refinement and stature the sentence was harsh.

The Yishuv treated Max as a hero. We all felt very proud of the boss. He was patently innocent, but we had learned not to trust the British. Their aim was to take Max out of circulation at a crucial time in the military and legal struggle over the White paper on the future of Palestine. They had wanted him to go to prison and had used the corruptible Gilpin to frame him.

Now from my point of view, leaving the office at such a critical time was not to be countenanced. I should have to remain in Palestine to hold the fort, while Mr. Seligman spent four months as a guest of the Government.

I immediately wrote to Leah to prevent her going to London, but it was too late. She had already made arrangements to be in London in August. Her reply was that she expected me to be there whatever happened. I fumed. That was just like Leah. I had been away from the States for five years and she still treated me like a child, expecting me to drop everything on her instructions. Did she not know that I was running an important legal office, that my boss was in prison, that no way could I leave Palestine at present?

Even if I had wanted to leave, all ships were booked well in advance. All planes leaving twice weekly to London were fully booked. With the darkening position between Germany and Britain, everybody was either going home for good or taking the last chance to visit their families. Who knew what the future held?

In one way I was relieved. Perhaps fate was giving me a second chance. I wrote to Maurice to keep him up to date with the news.

'I am not coming to London, and I don't feel I have the right to ask you to wait. I have to be honest and say that I am still terribly vague and indefinite. I was going to meet Leah in London, which seemed the best solution because then I would not be a tourist as I was last time. I would be able to see you in everyday surroundings and get to know you and your life. But right now things are upset and, although you always seem to be with me in thought, I cannot say that everything will be all right for us.'

The office was deluged with cables and letters of goodwill for Max Seligman from all over the world.

Amongst the post was an invitation for me. It was to attend a wedding. Mac, my first real love, was getting married in September to a girl I knew but did not much like. They had invited *me!*. I sent them a bouquet of flowers with my good wishes, but declined the invitation saying I would be out of town that weekend.

Leah was in London in August and made contact with Maurice and his family, who took to her immediately. I wrote a letter to them jointly, wishing Leah a good stay and suggesting she come to visit the family in Palestine.

I thought she was selfish being so near and yet so far. When Mama realized Leah was in England she burst into tears at the thought of not seeing her. And here I was, intending to live in London 'If a war doesn't break out'. Goodness knew when we would all be together again.

For Maurice's benefit I added that I would keep the show running for Max, but when he came out of prison in November I would find a replacement for myself and, if things were the same between us, I would leave for London.

In the meantime, I had to arrange for a passport and visa, then patch up my winter wardrobe so that the English winter would not get the better of me. I would mark time until I was on my way.

We sat by the radio waiting for war to be declared. Every time they postponed the misery of announcing it, our nerves got weaker, our faces more sour. We continued waiting, hoping against hope that it would not be.

After all the stress of the past weeks, I intended to take a four day break in Haifa before the Jewish High Holy Days. I had told my parents I was visiting friends, but in truth I wanted to be alone. It was the weekend of Mac's wedding.

The Teltch House Hotel in Haifa was set high on Mount Carmel amongst the pine woods. On Friday evening, after I unpacked my small case and luxuriated in a bath, I went down for dinner.

'Would you care to share my table?' A tall, bearded elderly man stood as I entered.

I hesitated, but he seemed very pleasant.

'Thank you. I will,' I said, sitting opposite him.

Shabbat candles were placed on a long table for anyone to light when the first star appeared.

'Would you light the Sabbath candles for me?' he asked. His accent was a mixture of European and American. 'I am a long way from home. Let me introduce myself. I am a Professor.' We shook hands.

'I'm Harriett Gold,' I said. 'Look, I am not married. My mother has always lit the candles for us. But I will do it tonight. I believe we need the blessing of the Almighty this week more than ever. The news is so bad.'

I went to the table and, alongside other guests, lit two candles before covering my eyes and reciting the Sabbath prayer. Then a gentleman guest recited Kiddush, blessed the wine and bread, with everyone joining in before saying a hearty 'Amen!'

I visibly blushed as I returned to my table. The Professor rose politely as I sat down.

'Are you visiting?' I asked.

'I am on a lecture tour.' He smiled. 'And, yes, I live in the States now. My family fled from Poland in 1935. We are all out, thank the Almighty.'

'My father was an émigré from Russia at the turn of the century,' I said. 'I was born in the States, but he brought me here five years ago.'

Before I knew it we were engrossed in conversation. We spent Saturday walking in the pine woods together. He was as wise as J.L. and I found an affinity talking to him, even though he was three times my age.

'As a Professor of Language, I am concerned with how words develop,' he expounded. 'Language adapts and changes constantly, but only when it is a living language. That is the miracle of Hebrew. Held by the sages and used for prayer, but hardly alive for thousands of years. And now, thanks to the perseverance of Eliezer ben Yehuda, a Hebrew dictionary was started to bring the language up to date. Ivrit, modern Hebrew, is an example of bringing an old language into the modern world. Did you know that the word for telephone is, in translation, 'speak far' - *Sach Rachock*?

'I made the effort to learn Hebrew when I came to Palestine. That's one I do know,' I said.

'You impress me with your zeal,' he said, then quoted, 'One people, one nation, one language!'

I found the subject fascinating as he gave me more examples of how words developed.

'For instance, the word *Tal* in Hebrew means *Morning Dew*. The abbreviation of the name of the Almighty is *Yah*. If one puts these two words together you get *Talya*'.

I loved the sound of it.

'It could be a girl's name. It's so pretty and has a beautiful translation in any language!' I exclaimed. I made up my mind then and there that if I ever had a daughter I would call her Talya.

During that weekend the General Overseas Service of the BBC kept us informed of current news on the hotel radio. Poland had been invaded by German forces on Friday, 1st September. That was the 'last straw'. Britain and France had mobilized.

In Britain an evacuation scheme was started to remove children away from the cities. On 2nd September, compulsory military service was introduced for all men in Britain aged between 18 and 41. Many British Jews living in Palestine immediately joined up. War was now inevitable.

On Sunday morning some time after eleven the British Prime Minister, Neville Chamberlain, announced that Britain was at war with Germany. That evening hotel guests and staff gathered around the radio to hear King George VI's speech rallying the Empire. His voice echoed around the dining room, his stammer necessitating long pauses before phrases. He was a courageous man who had stepped on to the throne on the abdication of his elder brother. We felt for him and were stirred by his words.

In Palestine, Ben Gurion said, 'We shall fight with the British as if there were no White Paper, and fight the White Paper as if there were no war.'

I ran up to my room, grabbed some hotel note-paper and scribbled:

'Maurice darling,

Have just heard the latest news. I've been, of course, quite upset! Please, please let me hear as soon as possible - just a word so I can know what is what - We are all praying for a speedy successful end. - Please darling - write - and tell me all is as well as can be expected. Our love to you all. I am with you every moment. May God grant that all this misery will soon be ended. I've come up here for four days - just for a change - it was almost impossible to go on. Have just heard the King's speech. By the way, where is Leah? I haven't heard a word from her!

Much love, Harriett.'

All hotel guests, including the Professor and myself, departed early next morning to get back to their posts and put their affairs in order. Although Palestine was not immediately affected by the war, we knew that stringent laws would come into force: rationing and more curfews; censorship of letters and messages, especially from England. It was to be some time before any of us knew what had happened to Leah over there, and whether she had returned safely to the States.

CHAPTER 21

Tel Aviv and Jerusalem (Autumn 1939)

The moment war was declared Arab attacks on Jewish targets in Palestine increased. We were used to it by now, but since bombs were going off in Jerusalem where Mattie and Esther lived we were especially fearful for them.

There was sudden panic about food shortages. Everybody bought up extra stocks to store away, just in case. Only when the Government published notices saying there was sufficient food for everyone did things calm down. That did not stop prices from soaring.

The Holy Days of Rosh Hashanah and Yom Kippur were very subdued. The Jewish New Year (5700) arrived the second week in September. We did not feel very festive as we gathered in Herzlia with our parents trying to make the best of it. It was a relief to them that Esther and Mattie, Sol and I all sat around their dining table for Yomtov.

Mama was still upset about not having seen Leah when she was in Europe. Now we had no idea where she was. A New Year's greeting had arrived from Rhea and Rose in the States, but it had been written before the outbreak of war and read that Leah was enjoying herself in London. Her three letters from London arrived, together with one from Maurice, just before Yom Kippur. Apparently they were getting on just fine together. I felt quite left out!

Not having up-to-date news was worrying, especially since we knew that all mail was being censored. Any information had to be prevented from reaching the enemy, particularly as

I was in Palestine where there were pro-German followers of the Grand Mufti.

'Don't worry,' said J.L, trying to cheer us up. 'Leah will be all right. America knows how to look after its citizens.'

'What if her boat is attacked - or even sunk?' we worried. The British liner 'Athenia' had been sunk by a German submarine in the first week of the war.

'We are all in the hands of the Almighty,' said J.L.

I stayed over for Yom Kippur to keep Mama company whilst my father spent the day in the synagogue. It gave me time to collect my thoughts about life, about Leah and the war, about Maurice, marriage and my future. The fast was a peaceful, holy day, and my private prayers were that I should be settled in my mind. Strangely, they were answered. By the time I returned to Tel Aviv I had set my heart on going to England.

Now that Max Seligman was incarcerated in prison, my work lessened in the office. The other partners had their own staff so they would not miss me that much. I contacted Millie Seligman to let her know my decision to leave Palestine and offered her my resignation. She was adamant that she would not accept.

'Harriett, you simply cannot leave the firm now.'

'But we only work half days. There is nothing to do here.'

'You must stay, at least until November when Max is out of prison. He needs you to run the office for him.'

'But I have to go to England!' I exclaimed.

'Please, Harriett. I am worried. What with Max imprisoned and everything.' She trailed off. 'Look, if you want a rise, you have it!'

'It's not that,' I said lamely. How could I explain that my mind was made up at last and I wanted to get on with my life *immediately*.

'Do you agree?' insisted Mrs. Seligman at the other end of the line.

'All right,' I sighed.

There was so little work to do that I organised a rota leaving just one employee in the afternoons to cover. When it was my turn, I spent the hours typing letters to Maurice. I had not heard from him since 1st September. Perhaps his letters had not passed censorship yet.

I knew some of the people who worked as censors and certainly I would not like them to read my intimate thoughts. I hinted as much to Maurice that I was going to be careful about what I wrote. My letters would be more stilted than ever. I hoped he would read between the lines.

'Why any man would like to receive a typed letter from his girl-friend beats me,' observed a young clerk on his way out past my desk.

'Why? When you have a lot to say, and when you mean what you say, what the hell's the difference?' I exploded.

'A short missive in your own fair hand is far better!' he threw back.

I sat looking at the half typed letter in the typewriter after he had left. In one way, it was true. My most intimate letters to Maurice had been written by hand. I slumped back in the chair. His love letters to me were beautifully hand-written and deeply expressive. He was a romantic. I knew I was a realist. Were we suited? What the hell! I was a secretary for heavens sake. My news and thoughts were easily put on paper through my fingers. As to my feelings, well, I had never been able to express them easily anyway. He could take Harriett Gold as he found her, or not at all.

The unbearable afternoon heat penetrated the office. I felt deflated and tired. I would finish the letter tomorrow. Maybe then I would feel more at ease with myself. I sure hated that clerk!

*

Esther and Mattie invited me to spend Succoth with them in Jerusalem. Their charming apartment was in a quiet residential area shaded by huge pines. It was good to see them so happily settled.

'I am going to visit Max in prison tomorrow,' I told them. 'They are keeping him in the central prison until November.'

'Will you be allowed in?' asked Esther.

'I believe so. Visiting concessions are made over the Jewish holidays. I am his secretary, after all.'

I presented myself in the afternoon, and was shown into a waiting room by a polite Arab warder who left the door open and assured me that Mr. Seligman would see me soon. The general noise of prison pervaded the atmosphere with shouts, distant commands and clanging doors. The sour smell of internment permeated the place.

I stood up when Max Seligman was ushered in and the door closed behind him. He looked paler and thinner, but surprisingly cheery.

'Hello Harriett! Why are you here and not in the office?'

He grinned and sat down opposite me, crossing his legs and looking very relaxed. On the other hand, I felt extremely nervous as I was deserting him at a very bad time.

'The office is fine,' I said, hesitating. 'I expect Millie has told you my news?'

He stared hard at me.

'I heard the great news,' he said sarcastically.

'I am twenty two. I am old enough to make up my own mind,' I said indignantly. 'Do you mind?'

He guffawed. 'Harriett. You can do whatever you like. I don't care if you marry or jump in the river. But you are not doing either until you have replaced yourself.'

I stared at him. He was amused by me.

'But I have to get to England!' I exclaimed.

'Now? During a war? You must be in love!'

I wanted to change the subject quickly.

'It is strange seeing you in here. How is it?' I enquired.

'As a lawyer, I have probably visited more prisons in Palestine than anyone, but believe me, one needs to be confined to know what conditions inside are really like.' He grimaced. 'It is quite a salutary experience, I can tell you. I share a cell with the only other three Englishmen in here. They are polite but openly anti-Semitic.

'I do have special privileges though. That means a bed of sorts instead of the floor. I can wear my own clothes, as you see. Otherwise, it is very primitive.'

'You look thinner. Have you been getting food sent in? And other things?' I mouthed.

I knew that the Arab warders were often bribed to smuggle in letters, messages or newspapers. Max had been kept up to date with outside news in this way. He nodded.

'Conditions in prison are not improved by the war, let me say. I won't frighten you with details. Naturally I wrote to the authorities volunteering to join the British Army, but doubtless the letter was never forwarded.'

He leaned towards me lowering his voice.

'But I am still working, even in here. Many prisoners, both Arabs and Jews, maintain their innocence and seek my help. I manage to slip into the cell where the majority of Jewish prisoners are held. I help them draft petitions, advise them, you know. It's against the rules, so if I am caught - well!'

He chuckled, then his face lit up.

'Life goes on nevertheless. Rabbi Arie Levin attends from outside the prison. He's a very kindly man, very encouraging. He brings messages and comfort to the prisoners from their families. He held Holy Day services in here and I was Cantor throughout Rosh Hashanah and Yom Kippur. I enjoyed it. We were a motley congregation.' He reflected on that thought. Then, 'Harriett, apart from your love-life, how are things outside?'

'Well, I should say that all social functions died a natural death when you were incarcerated, but Arnold and Queenie are still entertaining. We somehow manage to have fun,' I teased.

He laughed. 'You would!'

'Are there any messages?' I took out my notebook.

'I am going to appeal. I want you to go and see Yehuda Nedivi, Town Clerk of Tel Aviv. Ask him to be a character witness for me. Do you know him?'

I did not, but I had heard of him and promised to approach him on Max's behalf. He gave me other instructions for the office and messages of love for Millie and his children as the warder opened the door, stood to attention and waited for Max to finish.

'Take care of yourself, my girl,' he said on his way out. 'Wait until I get out of here, then you can advertise for your replacement. I doubt if you will find one because I am difficult to suit!'

*

Over the next few days the climate was unbearably hot. Going out of doors was like walking into the blast of a furnace. What with ominous news of the war, it felt as if the whole world was about to catch fire.

Every day we 'sat on the radio' waiting for news bulletins. The German invasion of Poland was gathering pace. Lodz had fallen. Russia was moving from the east in a pact to carve up Poland. God help the Poles, and in particular Polish Jews. We all knew the terrible threat they were under from what the boys in the Irgun had told us. It was a horrible waiting game.

We were appalled to learn that the Palestine Police were arresting German Jews who had managed to escape in time, and were guarding them in concentration camps on suspicion of being pro-Nazi spies.

For our part, any travel arrangements in Palestine were officially monitored or curtailed. I realised how lucky I had been to get safely back from Jerusalem now that travel was restricted to the military. There seemed no chance of my leaving for England.

Since I was stuck in Tel Aviv it was impossible to just sit around. I joined a First Aid class, graduated quickly and was able to pass on what I had learnt to younger girls. I also arranged to take driving lessons. I was determined to be able to drive so that I would be useful in whichever country I found myself.

Eventually at the beginning of October, Maurice's beautifully hand-written letter arrived. He had carried my note from Haifa, which reached him on the 17th September, in his pocket because it was 'the only ray of brightness in the present black-out'.

None of my other letters had reached him. He was deeply depressed. With impending war his business had flagged and was on the verge of bankruptcy. He had persuaded his partners to draw no salaries until debts were paid off. At last the factory was involved in the war effort manufacturing uniforms, eleven hours a day Monday to Friday and five hours on Sunday mornings. He was frantically busy, but although the weekly turnover was beginning to show a profit he felt the business would be a constant worry during the war. He wrote all this and added:

'It is difficult to look forward beyond tomorrow. It is difficult to believe that you will be able to come here in December, entirely apart from all questions of risk for you to come to London. Would it be selfish of me to hope that you will try?'

I was determined that I would. Not even a war was going to stop me now that I had made up my mind.

Maurice had no doubt that Leah would be safely back home by now. As soon as war was declared, she had been instructed to take the train to Scotland with other American nationals to be shipped back to the States away from the war zone. No other news of her was good news.

His long letter had been worth waiting for. All his reminiscences of Palestine tumbled across the page, half affectionately, half caustic.

'Tell me please, how are things in Palestine? Does the San Remo Hotel still stand where it was? Do the Yerushalmi and Galilea still sail between Haifa and Trieste discarding their passengers as regularly as ever? Do the German refugees still pollute the Zionist atmosphere with the blasphemous German language? Do the taxi men continue to try and squeeze the extra 50 miles from poor ignorant tourists? Is the Pilz still the centre of Bohemia and do the Army lorries rumble through the streets at all hours of the day and night? Does the sun still shine or do war clouds hang everywhere? And the orange juice - ah! the orange juice that was cheaper than water - does it still flow through the land of milk and honey? Does the Yemenite Jew still lie down on the pavement (preferably opposite Barclays Bank in Allenby Street) with all his household and go to sleep

*and does the eternal donkey still suffer the loads of man
and burden through the dry, dusty streets? Do the armies of
people still stand from morning till night, trying, by hook
or by crook, to get travel passes?*

*'The shop where I bought my films, Rothschild Boulevard,
the Habimah, the cinema, Esther's semi-American, semi-
Jewish sweetness - the sound of the sea from my bedroom.
Do cars still drive on the right hand side of the road, a
danger to every pedestrian, animal, bicycle, lamp-post,
policeman as well as to every other car! Tel Aviv!'*

He was describing my home, my land, my people. For the
first time, we were sharing it.

*'And how are you? Have you recovered now from all the
worry and muddle and do you feel much better? We Jews
are the most inveterate optimists ever. Despite all our
suffering and incredible troubles and heart-breaking
difficulties, we still have courage and hope and faith, and
we still wish each other a 'Happy New Year'; though we say
it with tears in our eyes, we still smile. When we come
across a fervent Catholic, Muslim, Buddhist, we say 'What
an amazing thing his religion must be, to be able to hold its
believers so firmly.' Would one say that of Judaism? Is it
our religion or our tradition, our history or our own
innate character that makes us so staunch? Goodnight and
God bless you. I hope that the New Year will be 'different' I
hope it will bring much happiness to you and to all your
family. Everything here is 'As well as can be
expected.'...Bless you again, Harriett....*

All my love, Maurice'

In his office on Sunday morning, 24th September, the first
Sunday of petrol rationing, feeling disappointed there was no
mail from me he added a postscript:

'*As I drove down to the City this morning, the roads were practically clear and very few buses were running. I cannot imagine how the public is expected to get about. I was stopped by three men who were waiting for a bus to take them City-wards and they asked me to give them a lift. I was pleased to do so. I expect plenty of that sort of thing will take place in future. My car is a 21 horsepower job and does 16/18 miles to the gallon: I have been allowed a ration of TEN gallons per MONTH! It won't take me to the office and home again for a fortnight!*

'*We have a kitten in the factory, a funny little thing. Its greatest amusement is climbing over tables, desks, cupboards, chairs and so on and it sits on the highest point it can find and licks itself. It follows me all over the building but always returns to the office. You know those wire baskets that one uses for papers, well, the kitten has just turned one into a bed-sitting room just at my side and is now sitting up and staring at me with the greenest, feline eyes I have ever seen.*'

All of a sudden I wanted to pick up and cuddle that little kitten in the office. I wanted to be with Maurice. I was going to get over to London, no matter what.

CHAPTER 22

Tel Aviv (November 1939)

In the office everyone eagerly looked forward to the imminent release of Mr. Seligman. The telephone hardly stopped ringing with enquiries from colleagues and friends who wanted to know when Max would be returning. It occurred to me that it would be wonderful to hold a welcome home party to give people a chance to see him. When I next spoke to his wife, Millie, I ventured the idea.

'We could have it here in the apartment,' she agreed. 'I'm sure it would give him enormous pleasure to have all his friends around him.'

'Just so that he knows how much he means to us,' I said. 'I'll be happy to help out. May I come round later to discuss food, drink and a guest list?'

'It could be a surprise party,' I suggested when we met that evening.

'Well, you know Max,' warned Millie. 'He is very perceptive. I may not be able to hoodwink him.'

'He hasn't been to the cinema for months. Why don't you suggest going to the movies with him. He'll buy that and it will keep him out of the way while I set up everything.'

Millie and I felt very conspiratorial but excited, making arrangements to book caterers, sending out invitations and organising the surprise.

I had another assignment which Max had requested. Next morning I telephoned the Town Clerk, Yehudi Nedivi, who suggested that I saw him at his home in Rothschild Boulevard after work that evening. He was a courteous, clean-shaven gentleman who opened the door for me when I arrived. He gently ushered me into his sitting room and sat down with me.

'Now, what can I do for you. er.. Miss?'

'Harriett Gold.' I extended my hand. 'I am here on behalf of Max Seligman.'

'A courageous man. I know him well,' he said.

'As you are aware, he is in prison at present - unjustly. He protests his innocence and wishes to appeal against the judgement.'

'Of course. I understand.' He nodded.

'He has suggested you might be one of his character witnesses.' I paused, warming to the subject. 'I am sure you realise that many of us have helped immigrants enter Palestine. You know he did what any decent Jew would do to help save people's lives. You know that nothing he did was criminal or corrupt.'

'Naturally. But how can I help?' He leaned forward and smiled.

'By the mere fact that you are who you are. I am certain your good account of him will carry much weight. He needs people to say he is a man of good character.'

He looked at me very intensely, then said, 'If I had someone to plead for me as you are doing for Max, I would consider myself a fortunate man, Miss Gold.'

I blushed.

'*Haray Aht,*' he pronounced my name like the first words of the marriage contract. 'My admiration for you in your faithfulness to Mr. Seligman is unbounded. Of course I shall do anything I can to fulfil your request.'

'Thank you.' I stood to leave.

'When does he come out? I expect he will be very relieved to have home comforts once more.'

'Oh yes! And we are giving him a surprise party,' I said eagerly before I could stop myself.

'Well, Haray Aht, I should very much like to be there,' said Yehuda Nedivi as he walked me to the door.

He was such a charmer that I made a mental note to put his name on the guest list.

*

On the morning of 7th November, crowds lined the streets outside the prison to throw flowers in front of the car carrying Max Seligman home to Tel Aviv. Millie was inundated with bouquets from organisations and friends. We left the two of them alone to have an emotional reunion.

Max telephoned the office almost at once.

'Harriett, I'm back!' he said.

'Oh good! See you tomorrow then.'

'Everything running well?' he enquired. 'Oh, Millie is telling me to let you know I'm going out this evening to the movies. So I'm back in the swing. We're going to see Deanna Durbin in *That Certain Age*.'

'You will love it! Enjoy yourself. You deserve it,' I said.

We had arranged to have him out of the way by five thirty, when I would go around to the flat to let in the caterers with the cold buffet and drinks. Everything went according to plan. By seven thirty all the guests were excitedly assembled. A look-out was posted on the balcony to give the signal.

'They're coming!' he said in a loud stage whisper.

The lights were turned off and everyone fell silent. We could hear ourselves breathing. Then footsteps outside and a key being turned in the lock.

'Surprise!' we yelled, switching on the lights and beaming at our hero.

211

Max was completely taken aback. He stood with his hands over his eyes for a second, then someone stepped forward and handed him a glass of champagne and the party took off. It was wonderful to have him back.

'You know the story of the poor students who were always hungry?' joked Max, drawing on his Player's cigarette and waving it in the air. 'Whenever they heard there was a function in town, be it a wedding or Barmitzvah, they gate-crashed and ate to their hearts' content.'

'Any students here?' yelled somebody.

Everybody laughed happily while Max continued.

'The caterer's staff complained there was no food left over to take home. This was strange because they always over catered and overcharged. Eventually they realised it was due to the uninvited guests. So from then on the caterers posted someone at the door. If it were a Barmitzvah he'd ask, 'Are you on the side of the bride or the groom?' And if it were a wedding he would ask the name of the Barmitzvah boy! That way, he soon discovered who were the interlopers. 'Out!' he shouted. 'This is a Barmitzvah - not a wedding!' - or 'It's a wedding, not a Barmitzvah!''

Max smiled benignly at us.

'So that's how I feel tonight. Like a student at the wrong party!'

He looked around at our beaming faces.

'But I am over the moon to see all my friends and colleagues,' he added. 'Now I want to hear all the new jokes!'

Everybody was very happy, which made it a good party. Max had more energy than all of us. He danced and joked more than anyone. We celebrated until midnight. Then, when most of the guests had gone and we had discussed them all, an intimate group of us went on to the Hinga Night Club in

Guela Street where we danced away the rest of the night with Millie and Max.

It was a mark of Max's stamina and my commitment to the job that we both arrived at the office at the same time next morning.

'Come into my office,' said Max, striding in to the pile of documents on his desk. Within the hour he had dictated answers to back-dated correspondence and examined legal documents.

'Good Lord!' he exclaimed as he held up an Affidavit. 'Judge Curry hears my client's case today. I shall enjoy appearing before him. He's the judge who convicted me!'

Only minutes later he was out of the office on the way to court to face a nonplussed but courteous judge. Once again he was able to obtain judgement for his client. Max was back.

*

Now that I had Max Seligman's permission to replace myself and train up a new girl, there was nothing to prevent me from joining Maurice in London. I placed an advertisement in the newspaper which read: 'Experienced Shorthand/Typist with excellent English as Secretary to Senior Partner in busy Law Office. Full time. Well paid. Start immediately.'

Several applicants came to me for interviews, but none seemed to have the experience or flexibility that I knew Max would need.

'I'll keep trying,' I told him. 'I am also trying to organise my exit visa. The U.S. government have said they won't allow their nationals to move into a belligerent area, so I was thinking of applying for a British passport. I am a Palestinian now, after all! What do you think?'

'I think you're crazy,' replied Max. 'I won't stop you though. You are unstoppable once you have made up your mind!'

When I presented myself to the American Consulate in Tel Aviv, I was told sarcastically that England was at war with Germany. My application for a visa was refused.

'But I am getting married!' I exclaimed to the Embassy official.

'Perhaps your future husband will come here to marry you?'

'How can he?' I exclaimed. 'He is at war!'

'Exactly,' muttered the clerk.

Oddly enough, these genuine impediments to my leaving Palestine made me quite determined to go. I reacted angrily to being thwarted yet again in my plans to marry my Englishman.

'Harriett, I don't like the thought of you leaving for a war zone,' Mama said when I recounted my frustration. 'Perhaps it is right that they won't grant you a visa.'

'Well I don't know how I feel about going into a war area either,' I said. 'But if I get there, then there I will be - and then I will know!'

I wrote to Maurice suggesting he might be able to pull some strings in London to get me a visa. Between us, we would see a way through.

Esther and Mattie celebrated their first anniversary on 3rd November. It seemed incredible how time had flown. I did not join the celebrations because we agreed mother should go to visit them in Jerusalem and I offered to stay with J.L.

'Do you want to marry this man?' asked my father in his straightforward way when we were together.

'Yes,' I said. 'Preferably before he gets called up for active service.'

214

'Then you will be alone in a strange land,' he warned.

'Papa, you were once alone in a strange land. Look, I just want to be ready so that when I want to leave I can just pack up and go. Let's wait to see what time will bring.'

'I brought you up to have a mind of your own, so I won't argue with you. I'll help in whatever way I can. You know that.'

'Well, obtaining a visa is one difficulty,' I said.

'Leave it to me,' said J.L. with assurance. 'I shall write to Mr. Stimson, Secretary of State in Washington, and explain your predicament. Since you will acquire British Citizenship immediately upon your marriage, the government of the United States will relinquish any responsibility for your security. I don't believe they will refuse you a visa.'

I had great confidence in my father's ability to sort things out and returned to Tel Aviv feeling much happier.

A letter awaited me from someone I had never met. It was from Maurice's mother and read:

Nov 2nd 1939

Dear Harriett,

Both Mr. Goodman and I are extremely happy to hear that you intend coming to London and we are already looking forward to meeting you.

I would like to mention how much I enjoyed the company of your sister when she was over here, and I was really sorry when she left.

I hope that you and your parents are keeping well. Please give them our kindest regards and our assurance that, when you come here, we shall take great care of you just as if you were our own child.

Looking forward to seeing you soon,
With love and best wishes,
Ettie Goodman.

I was pleased to hear from his folks. It added to my certainty that all would turn out well in the end.

Next morning a letter from Maurice informed me that he had visited the American Embassy in London to make a statement that we were to be married. He thought this should do the trick. It seemed to work because a few days later I got a letter from the immigration department in Tel Aviv requesting that I go and see them.

The Inspector of Immigration turned out to be a friend of mine, Mr. Wolfson.

'Hello, Harriett. Please do sit down,' he said. 'I have asked to see you because I want to be the one to tell you that I have had instructions to give you a permanent visa for England.'

'That's wonderful!' I exclaimed. 'I have a letter from Mrs. Goodman, if you wish to see it.'

'No. That won't be necessary. However, I need to see your passport. Do you have it with you?'

I did, and handed it over expectantly for the visa to be stamped on it.

'I am sorry, my dear, this is not valid.' He returned it to me. 'You will have to get it renewed by the American Consulate.'

'So I shall have to go to Jerusalem? Another impediment! Then will I get my visa?'

'I am sure you will.' He stood to show me out. 'Good luck and be happy!'

The American Consulate in Jerusalem was closed when I arrived. It was Thanksgiving Day, which I had quite forgotten. I stayed over the weekend with Esther and Mattie. They were very happy together and since they were the only married couple in their crowd of friends, everyone always gathered at their home. They did not have a moment to themselves. It was wonderful to see that Esther was simply adored by everyone who knew her.

On Monday morning I tried the Consulate again. This time I was able to pay my renewal fee and fill out a form saying why I wanted my passport renewed at this time.

'This is all in order,' said the girl placing a RENEWAL stamp across the passport. She then picked up another stamp.

'What is that one for?' I asked.

'It says THIS PASSPORT IS NOT VALID IN ANY COUNTRY OF EUROPE'

'What! I object!' Now I was very angry.

She held the stamp in mid air.

I fumed. 'That is absurd! Putting it on my passport when the renewal form states very specifically that I am intending to leave for Great Britain in the immediate future!'

'I think you had better speak to the American Consul, Mr. Minor, and explain your position to him,' she said sweetly.

'I will do just that!' I exploded.

Mr. Minor was a charming man who listened very sympathetically before calling in the clerk with the stamp and stamping my passport himself.

'But!' I jumped up in protest.

'Sit down, Miss Gold, so that I can explain our position. Congress has passed a law stopping all and any Americans from travelling to Europe unless it is a matter of life and death.'

'It is a matter of my future life,' I said pointedly.

'Yes, I understand. But think. Should any American traveller be hurt it would make complications. The American Government do not feel that any one person is worth getting all the rest of America involved in the European conflict.'

'I am perfectly willing to travel at my own risk. I am not asking the American Government for their protection. I am getting married to an Englishman!'

'That does not interest us. We do not want anyone travelling into a war zone. And marriage is not a sufficiently urgent reason for going to Europe at the present moment.'

'I was promised that in the event of all my papers being in order I would be allowed to travel. Now you are going back on your word.'

'Miss Gold, at that time I had not received these further instructions. Look, I am going to let you see this official document.'

He handed me a telegram. I grudgingly read the cable. It stated that every passport, without exception, must be stamped unless permission was granted by the State Department, Washington. All his arguments were quite logical and besides the stamp was already in my passport, so I appealed to his better nature and asked what he could suggest.

He shook his head.

'And what if I wanted to return to America?' I queried.

'In that event I will make your passport valid for whichever port you have to touch on your way back.' He looked seriously at me. 'But I am sure you do not intend to go to America via England. And even if you do, I would have to object as that is not the simplest or safest way to go at the moment.'

This was a fight that I was not prepared to lose.

'What shall I do?' I looked at him despairingly.

'The only thing I can suggest is that you get a British visa stamped on the passport. If you succeed in obtaining that, together with a French Transit visa, you may get a travel agent to sell you a ticket on the strength of that, and you would have no further worry. You could leave when you liked.'

'I shall appeal to the American Government!'

'You would have to cable America, which would cost about $20, giving all your information, and I am sure the answer will still be no. Last week the State Department refused a very important man permission to leave Palestine. And if you want to appeal in writing, that will take at least three months, and I am still sure they will refuse. I am sorry I cannot help you, my dear, but believe me it is for your own good.'

I returned to the office feeling very depressed.

*

The first rain came in the middle of November. The temperature dropped suddenly and it was freezing all day. The weather matched my mood. It also made me realise the British climate when I arrived was going to be changeable and wintry. I would have to reassess my wardrobe.

In the meantime I found a replacement for my office position. She was Ruth, a German-born immigrant the same age as I, with excellent English and very good secretarial skills.

'Please start next Monday and I will teach you the ropes,' I said. 'Then when I get my permission to leave, I'll be off straight away.'

Ruth was very efficient. I gave up my desk to her and was therefore able to ease myself out without any disturbance to the running of the office.

'I have no complaints about Ruth,' said Max when I told him I would leave quite soon. 'But I shall miss you, Harriett. Over the years I have watched you grow up. But I know you will enjoy London, and I shall make a point of keeping in touch with you whenever I am there.'

'If I ever get there,' I sighed, recounting the difficulties spelt out by the American Ambassador.

'Look, you have been resident in Palestine for five years, under the British Mandate. Do what he suggests. Try to obtain a British visa stamp and if I can help with a character reference, I will.' He chuckled. 'A strong character reference!'

CHAPTER 23

The Settlements (1939-1940)

The festival of Chanukah was again being celebrated in the streets of Tel Aviv. I walked along with the throng to cheer the runner lighting the first candle of the Chanukiah, before the torch was carried to Jerusalem.

'I've been here five years and each time the festival, like the miracle of the lights, holds more significance for me. It gets bigger,' I thought, wondering when or if I should ever see them again.

That evening I joined a dinner party at the Talpiot Hotel with my dear friends, Zippora and Alec, Molly and Jack. Eli was also with them. He and I had met several times over the past month in the company of others, but we had not enjoyed any more quiet reflective evenings together. These days it did not upset me to be in his company. I was occupied with other plans for my future.

'Just when are you leaving us, Harriett?' asked Molly.

'I honestly don't know at the moment. When I know, you will know.'

'What's the hold-up?' asked Alec.

'I can't get a visa,' I said. 'The USA won't let me go to Britain until the war is over.'

'Well, that might take some time!' said Eli sarcastically.

I ignored him.

'I have applied for a British visa. Without one I can't renew my passport or get a French transit visa, or even book a place for leaving. Everything depends on when it comes. I wish I knew a way of getting round it,' I said.

'I have a suggestion,' said Eli, leaning back in his chair and giving me a long hard look. I raised my eyebrows.

'Marry me. Then you'll get a British passport.'

I smiled sweetly.

'You're too late!' I replied.

'You could marry by proxy,' suggested Alec. 'If you marry a Britisher you automatically become British and could join your husband without any trouble.'

'She's not to even think of that!' Zippora was indignant. 'Harriett, you just could not do such a thing – without being there under the Chupa, properly blessed.' She turned to Alec and held his hand.

'I won't. But if things don't work out, I may have to get an Italian visa and go that way.'

'I can't bear the thought that we will not be at your wedding,' she sighed.

All of a sudden I felt tearful.

'How am I going to live without you all?' I said.

'How are we going to live without you!' they chorused.

At the end of the week I went again to the Immigration office to re-submit my application. Incredibly, the clerk did not notice the prohibitive stamp on my passport.

'Your passport will be sent to Jerusalem and you should receive it in about ten days. Your application has also to get CID clearance,' he said. 'Do you have a criminal background?'

'No I do not! But if I don't get my visa soon I shall feel like killing somebody!' I replied.

My first love, Mac, appeared one morning in the office on some pretext.

'Hello Harriett. I have just heard you are leaving for England. Is that true?' He hovered around my desk.

'It is true. How are you, Mac? And your wife?'

'Are you planning to go on to America? Or stop in England?' he enquired, without mentioning her.

'Is that a tactful way of finding out whether I'm planning to take the plunge?'

'Well, I just wondered.'

'Just how is married life?' I persisted.

'Yes, yes it is good,' he said. 'But it's very strange. Every evening I feel I should be going 'home'.

'Well, aren't you?'

'Not to mother,' he said.

When he left the office, I just laughed aloud at my lucky escape.

I impatiently awaited news of the visa. In the meantime I looked up all the routes I could take on my way out and sent the information to Maurice. By boat it would cost £48 first class to Trieste £32 second class. The train from Trieste to Paris second class cost £8, and to fly from Paris to England cost £8. All excluding food on the way. Going by boat would take much more time, so I was seriously considering flying. There would be a certain amount of danger in any kind of travelling whichever way I went, but I decided not to think about that.

If I travelled by plane the luggage restriction was 20 kilos, so I should be able to take only absolute essentials. My precious books and pictures, most of my clothes and mementoes would all have to be left behind. I would have to arrange for Esther to send those on to me when I was married.

As for being settled, just where was I going to live? Not in the house Maurice had occupied with his girlfriend, that was for sure. I wrote as tactfully as I could.

'Maurice dear – about the house – I really have so little knowledge of how large your house is – nor have I any idea of how one does live in England – or where or anything else. All I can say is that with my great knowledge of running a home and with all there is still for me to learn (and I'm willing) I certainly think that a flat is a much better idea. Besides Maurice dear, I've been living in places furnished by other people for such a long time – I would really like to have something that was like myself – chosen by myself and mine own.'

In the next post a letter arrived from the American Embassy in Jerusalem stating that my application for permanent visa to reside in England had been sent to the United Kingdom for approval. To date, no acknowledgement had been received.

'Now it is only a matter of a little more patience and all will be well,' I told myself. I decided it was time to give two week's notice to Max Seligman.

On my final day, everybody seemed very sad. I felt miserable leaving so many good friends, all of whom gave me parting gifts.

'Millie and I would like you to accept this,' said Max handing me a beautiful silver salver. 'And never be a stranger to us.'

'I shall treasure it always,' I said, with a lump in my throat. 'You will come and see me when you are in London, won't you?'

'Of course. You are part of the family,' he said.

Now that I was no longer bound by work, I seemed to be more rushed than ever. I bought a trunk in which to put clothes and precious items to be forwarded. My trousseau was laid out in apple pie order ready to pack into the one case I was allowed to fly with. My friends were in constant touch, ever inviting me around for farewell dinners.

Every day I expected to receive confirmation that my visa had been granted, then I would immediately be able to obtain travel tickets. It was time to leave my apartment and move into a hotel. By the New Year I wanted to be ready to up and go within a week of receiving permission.

In the last week of December I wrote to Maurice:

'I am at the office now – if I didn't come in here to write letters I just would never get them done. I do hope that when I get there I will be near a typewriter occasionally – or otherwise just think of my poor family pining away for want of letters from their darling little Harriett – oh it just breaks my heart to think of it. Rather funny what a year will bring – and well, my darling, it is just one year since you were here – oh what a year – but it has passed and here am I still smiling and very much alive – so it seems it will take an awful lot to kill me. As soon as there is the least bit of news I promise to cable.'

The weather had turned intermittently wet and stormy but everything in my life was beginning to fall into place.

At the weekend I carried my wedding dress home in a box to show my parents. With it were several yards of veil which Mama was going to arrange on to a headband with artificial orange blossom. My dress, which I designed myself, was fashioned in pure silk velvet, with sun-ray panels radiating from the bodice and a gathered taffeta band at the hem to make the panels stand out. It had a demure high-collar and long sleeves with tiny buttons right to the elbow. I stood in front of my bedroom mirror admiring the way it showed off my slender figure.

'You look lovely,' said Mama, as she arranged the veil to be short at the front to cover my face before the ceremony and very long at the back to make a train.

Papa stood in the doorway.

'Maurice should be very proud of you,' he said coming in to admire me.

That weekend my father had received a reply to his letter of appeal to the Secretary of State giving me permission to travel, on the condition that I was to report to the American Embassy in London on arrival and hand in my passport. The implication was that they would then have no responsibility for my waywardness. J.L. looked a little concerned.

'Just remember what you are letting yourself in for,' he warned. 'Until this war ends we will not see one another. You will not be able to come back.'

'Well the war will end and then you *will* come back. In the meantime, you will be making a home and starting a new life. You won't have time to travel,' said Mama wisely.

'I don't know how long I will be away, but you can be certain I'll be back,' I promised. 'Wouldn't it be wonderful if Maurice came to live over here with me? We could look for an apartment in Jerusalem together, or maybe Haifa. I am going there with Esther next week to find a place for her and Mattie, since his job will be in Haifa.'

'You may like to settle here in Herzlia,' dreamed Mama. 'This will always be your home.'

The last week in December was spent in Jerusalem with Esther, Mattie and Sol.

'I'm going up to Hanita next week,' said Sol. 'Would you like to tour around before you leave?'

'Yes please. I have no idea if or when I can return to Palestine,' I said. 'I want to see all the latest kibbutzim established in areas never before lived in or even cultivated. To me they are miracles of faith.'

Early in 1940 I retraced my journey to visit the settlements. My trip around the country was something extraordinary. I had the most glorious time.

Beyond Safed, there were no paved roads or paths. Trucks rumbled us around the whole area, picking up new friends on the way. We went to all the newest settlements and spent a night in each. We revisited Hanita, where we stayed overnight before moving on to Dafna. In the company of my warm-hearted, beloved brother, Sol, I saw again the commitment of pioneers.

What amazed me was that although inside the perimeter fence many things for living were still very primitive (there were no proper toilets, no real homes - and electricity from a small generator was only used for special things), they had taken the trouble to create a stage out of a hillside where the mouth of the river Dan flowed. It was important to them that they keep their cultural life alive. Once they had their open air theatre, drama and theatrical groups could visit to give performances. To think of it! Musical recitals, even Shakespeare, performed in the rarefied evening air, miles from the city, for the dedicated Chalutzim.

We visited an old settlement called Ayelet Hashochar, which means Rising of the Morning Star. After Hanita and Dafna it seemed luxurious, even though they truly had very little. There was still no running water or flushing toilets. But

I had never seen such beauty. Large, open spaces stretching to the horizon. We awoke very early in the morning and sat outside together to watch the sun rise. The air was like soft gossamer; blue with clearness, sweet and pure as clean air can be. I breathed in deeply, experiencing the joy of freshly scented morning air. I knew I would never forget it.

*

On my return, a cable from Maurice informed me that he had organised a visa allowing me to travel directly to England. Everything should now proceed smoothly. My passport was in perfect order and valid until 30th April, 1940. My exit permit was valid until 5th April. If I left before the 5th and arrived in England before the end of April, all would be well.

There were two last formalities to complete. On cabled instructions from Maurice I had to obtain a certificate from the Beth Din to confirm that I was unmarried. I also called at the District Commissioner's office to publish notice of my forthcoming marriage. I was assured that after fourteen days the certificate from the District Commissioner would be ready. I hoped and prayed that this would be the last formality and that immediately upon receipt I would be able to leave to join Maurice 'when we can at last do the right thing by one another!'

I had been intending to leave for such a long time that many of my acquaintances were wondering if such a person as Maurice existed at all, or was it all in Harriett's imagination? When I finally left, I would not believe it myself.

I moved into the Talpiot Hotel and arranged my itinerary. There were no direct flights from Palestine to England. The travel agent advised that if I wished to fly I should do so from Lydda Airport to Cairo; then from Alexandria to Rome; from Rome to Le Bourget and across the channel to England. All travel would be hazardous, but this would be the quickest way. The only problem was that I would now need a visa to travel through France, which again the US Government would be unlikely to agree to. However, by now they were well aware of my case, and when I applied I was assured that the French visa would be issued sometime in March.

This final delay in my leaving upset me even more because I had packed winter clothes and it seemed that I should not arrive until the springtime. I would have to rearrange my wardrobe for packing.

I poured out my frustrations to Zippora who laughed at me.

'All Harriett is worried about is what to wear!' she teased.

'It is not that,' I said. 'It takes my mind off everything else I don't want to think about.'

Zippora sighed. 'I suppose you know what you are doing.'

'It is fate,' I said. 'But how can I forget Palestine and all it has come to mean to me?'

'You leave the past and start looking forward,' said Zippora. 'But you will never forget Palestine. You will always carry it in your heart, wherever you go. And look, I want you to have this as a wedding present.'

She held up one of her oil paintings of Jerusalem bathed in golden sunlight.

'I will take the canvas from the frame and you can roll it up in your luggage. Then you will be taking a little part of Palestine with you.'

We hugged each other in lifelong friendship, and promised we would meet again.

CHAPTER 24

Journey to England (1940)

All my family came to the airport at Lydda to see me off. My parents, Sol, Esther and Mattie linked arms with me for a farewell photograph in front of the aeroplane on the runway. The thought of leaving everyone behind suddenly caught at my throat and I began to sob.

'Now, no crying,' said Mama. 'There's no need to be upset. When the war is over we can see each other. It is not like when I left Russia. I never knew if I would ever see my parents again.'

'As long as we have our health and can afford to travel,' added my father. 'We will meet again quite soon, when we win this war.'

I was about to fly away, but I instinctively knew they were right. After I was married I *would* see my family again – all of them, in Palestine and the States. I might even have children to introduce to them, who knew?

Esther produced a delicate lace handkerchief which she pressed into my hand.

'This is not for crying,' she said. 'It is something borrowed. So you will have to hand it back to me one day.'

I fought back the tears and hugged my wonderful kid sister.

'Be happy,' we both said to one another.

With last kisses all round I boarded the aircraft to fly to Cairo. As the propellers began to turn and we taxied for take-off, I looked out of the little window and waved to the small family group who meant so much to me. We lifted into the sky and I watched the familiar terrain banking away and spanning out to yellow desert below me.

'I'll be back,' I promised myself.

*

There was a complete interchange of social relationships between the Jewish community in Palestine and the Egyptian Jewish community, all under the British Mandate. So it was that on arrival at Cairo airport I was met by kind friends of my parents, with whom I stayed overnight.

The next morning I was driven to 'Half-Way House' where a chauffeur driven Rolls Royce was waiting to drive me to Rebecca's parents' home in Alexandria, a very sophisticated city. Rebecca and I had become great friends in Tel Aviv. She came running out to greet me, introducing me to her parents, who were very well-to-do and lived in a grand house.

Servants laid out my dress for dinner as Rebecca came into my bedroom.

'May I see your wedding dress?' She sat on the bed. 'Aren't you just so excited?'

'I'm more nervous of the long journey ahead,' I said, unlocking my case where I had so carefully packed my clothes.

'Panels of softest velvet,' admired Rebecca holding up my wedding dress. 'Oh, Harriett, you will make such a beautiful bride!'

'It is strange, but I can hardly believe it is happening to me,' I mused.

'You are so lucky!' said Rebecca. 'What an adventure!'

'I have to get to England first,' I reminded her. 'The Dutch Airline KLM touch down in Alexandria on their way back from the East Indies. They have reserved a place for me and know where I am staying tonight. I hope they remember to send for me when the aeroplane arrives tomorrow.'

The four-engine airliner carried thirty-two passengers from Alexandria to Rome. On boarding we were advised that this aircraft, which was packed with Dutch passengers, was on its final journey from Dutch East Indies to Europe. In view of the war situation, they were taking their personnel home.

I was shown to my seat, which was an individual armchair with wooden arms. I placed my elephant hide cabin case, a gift from Esther and Mattie, under my chair and made myself comfortable. I had not experienced travel sickness on the earlier flight so I was not expecting to feel ill this time either.

The engines revved and accelerated before we rose into the air, then settled into a steady drone. First stop Rome, then Paris, then London. I promised myself I would enjoy the rest of my journey towards my new life.

As we flew out over the Mediterranean there was a sudden bump and a lurch. My stomach flew into my mouth but I was determined not to succumb. I closed my eyes, tried to relax and drifted into a dream where Maurice and Mama, J.L. and Esther were all standing under the wedding canopy with me.

'Wishful thinking!' I told myself, as I awoke with a start to feel the thrust of the aircraft taking me farther away from my folks, and nearer to my 'husband'.

After several hours in the air I felt very hemmed in, but did not dare stand up to stretch my legs for fear of being sick. When the aircraft was at last on Italian ground, rolling towards the terminal, we were advised to remain in our seats. But several passengers, equally weary of sitting so long, left their seats and stood up. As I raised myself into the gangway the moving aircraft suddenly lurched to the left and I fell backwards, catching my back on the wooden arm-rest. For a moment I felt a searing pain which gradually subsided. I thought no more about it.

I carried my cabin case through customs where my passport was hardly glanced at. Our coach passed the Forum and Colosseum on its way to the Excelsior Hotel where we were to have dinner and spend the night. I recalled Miss Gallagher's lessons, and thought I should try to visit Ancient Rome if I could find an hour before continuing my journey. But during the evening the pain in my lower back increased until I was in agony. I wondered if I had broken anything because it was difficult to walk and impossible to sit.

'You had better let a doctor see you,' advised one of the aircrew who was staying with us.

A kindly Italian doctor was found. He examined me in my room and assured me that nothing was broken.

'Your coccyx is bruised. You will be in discomfort for some days, but these tablets should help reduce any acute pain. The best remedy is to lay flat on your back for two days.'

'That will be impossible because I am travelling on to England,' I said.

'Try not to carry anything heavy,' he advised.

'I will, and thank you.' I lay back on the bed. The painkillers began to take effect and I drifted into sleep.

I managed to hobble downstairs next morning when, during breakfast, I was informed by a KLM representative that the flight to Paris was no longer available.

'Paris has been declared an open city,' he said. 'That means no aircraft is allowed into its air space. In view of the war in the East, we feel it best to accompany you to Paris by train and then put you safely on an Imperial Airways flight to England.

'Well, at any rate I am in Europe,' I thought. 'If I cannot get to London, then Maurice will simply have to come to Rome to marry me!'

The train journey from Italy was going to be very uncomfortable for me so I dosed myself with codeine to dull the pain. Resigned to the long journey, I carried a book to read called 'The Good Companions' by J.B. Priestley. As the train sped through France, my travelling companions - two Dutch passengers from the plane and two KLM flight crew – who were making their way back to Holland, spent time discussing the present wartime situation. I buried my head in my book, but could not avoid hearing what they said.

'The impressive might of the Third Reich will be hard to hold back,' said the pilot sitting opposite me. 'They have overrun Czechoslovakia and Poland with no opposition. They have signed a non-aggression pact with the Soviets to keep Russia off their backs. I hope to God they don't turn towards us.'

'The Germans respect us. We Dutch are a peace-loving people,' said my neighbour.

I could not help interjecting.

'The Jews are a peace loving people,' I said. 'It is awful what the Nazis are doing to them!'

I do not suppose, because of the way I looked - blonde, blue eyed and not the least like the wicked propaganda stereotype emanating from the Nazis – that any of them suspected I was Jewish.

The co-pilot snorted at my remark.

'The Nazis are not doing their job properly,' he sneered, sounding sinister.

'What do you mean?' I asked.

He smiled straight at me.

'They are not killing Jews fast enough,' he said.

It was as if he had punched me in the face. I was incensed. In an hysterical fury I rose out of my seat and tried to hit him, but my neighbour held me back.

'Miss Gold, he is not worth it. I assure you the Dutch don't feel like that. The man is despicable.'

The Nazi Dutchman vacated his seat and disappeared, followed by the pilot. But I was so distressed and disturbed by this first overt anti-Semitism I had ever encountered that I began to cry bitterly. It was proof positive for me that my father was right. Jewish Statehood had to come to fruition, and quickly, to fight such evil hatred.

The younger travelling companion declared, 'I am Dutch and I don't believe what the Nazis are doing is right.'

He left his seat and minutes later returned with a white jewellery box within which was a silver compact.

'Miss Gold. I would like you to have this as an apology for that disgraceful Dutchman. I shall report him to head office when we get back to Holland.' He held out the powder compact. 'I was bringing this as a gift for my sister, whom I haven't seen for seven years. I feel she will be happy to know why I have given it to you.'

'I could not think of it,' I said, blowing my nose and feeling very touched by his gesture. 'Thank you, I appreciate it, but I could not accept.'

'Please,' he insisted. 'It will be a token of what true Dutchmen feel for the Jews.'

'You are both very kind gentlemen,' I said, feeling it would be churlish to refuse the gift. 'I shall treasure it. Please let me have your names. I shall write them in my book 'The Good Companions', because that is what you are.'

On arrival in Paris, we parted. I was taken to the Hotel George V, where I went immediately to bed feeling extremely ill from taking too many tablets. I lay in a stupor just wanting to go back home.

Next day I managed to pull myself together to commence the last stage of the journey. I was entirely in the hands of KLM, who found me a seat on a flying boat from France to Poole.

This final passage was the worst. The flying boat hit one air pocket after another. By the time we landed and disembarked I had been sick for hours. I looked so green that the customs officer only gave my passport a cursory look then offered to assist me to the waiting coach. I had left Palestine on 1st April and arrived on English soil on 5th April. My journey was nearly over.

The clear crisp air of London in springtime revived me. As we drove through the streets, it was an entirely different city from the one I remembered. It seemed darker and dirtier. There were sandbags stacked against walls and around entrances. Windows of large buildings were criss-crossed with tape, or blacked out completely. On every street there were men and women in uniform.

The coach set us down at Airways House, Victoria. Now all I had to do was make contact with Maurice. He knew I was on the way, but had no idea of exactly when I would be arriving. I found a public telephone but I did not have any English coins. I looked around helplessly.

'Need any help?' A soldier came up to me, dropping the bulky kit bag he was carrying over his shoulder.

'I don't have any English money,' I said. 'And I need to call my fiancé.'

'Have it on me, luv. It's only tuppence!' He put his hand into his pocket and handed me the coins before turning to leave.

That small kindness made me feel good to be back in London.

I dialled the number of Maurice's office but was disappointed to find he was not there.

'Well, I am out of change for another phone call,' I said curtly to the girl who answered.

'You can make a reverse charge call. Do you have his home number?'

'No, I have his mother's number.'

'I am sure she will be glad to hear from you.' Was that his secretary speaking? I slammed the phone down and contacted his mother.

'Hello, Mrs. Goodman? It's Harriett. Is Maurice there?'

'My dear! It is good to hear from you. No, Maurice is not in. Where are you?

'I'm at Victoria. Shall I take a taxi to you?'

'No, dear. Take a taxi to the Grosvenor. I will book you a room.'

'Do I need a taxi? The Grosvenor is nearby,' I said.

'No! No!' Mrs. Goodman sounded very agitated. 'Not *that* Grosvenor – you can't possibly stay in Victoria! You want the Grosvenor House Hotel in Park Lane.'

'Please tell Maurice I've reached my destination,' I said, thinking *'At long last!'*

'I shall come to the hotel immediately,' said Ettie Goodman. 'Mr. Goodman will let Maurice know where you are - when we can find him.'

'Some welcome!' I thought, and went to hail a taxi cab.

I was first to arrive at the hotel. I booked myself in, but when the receptionist asked for my passport I refused to hand it over.

'It has to be surrendered to the American Consulate the minute I arrive,' I explained.

The manager was called over. He was understanding but adamant.

'I am certain you will not be deported overnight. You will have your passport returned tomorrow, Madam. In the meantime we will have your luggage taken to your room. Is there anything else you would like sent up?'

I wanted to say 'Pickled cucumbers would be good!' But instead I whispered, 'Tea, thank you.'

After I unpacked my clothes, I wrapped myself in my blue dressing gown and ran a bath. I was still not feeling at all well and the thought of a reunion with Maurice made me feel worse. There was a knock on the door.

'If it is Maurice, who cares!' I thought. 'He has seen me like this before.'

'Come in,' I called from the bed.

A tall, well-built lady with red hair entered.

'Hello Harriett. I'm Maurice's mother. It is so good to meet you at last,' she said, extending her hand.

I winced as I stood to shake hands. She looked concerned.

'Are you all right?' She squeezed my hand and helped me sit down.

'When the plane landed I stood up too soon. It jerked to a halt and I hit my back on the wooden arm of my chair.'

'You poor girl!' she sympathised. 'We must call a doctor.'

'The doctor in Rome assured me it was only bruised and to lie flat for two days.'

'Nevertheless, we must be sure,' she insisted. 'May I?'

She picked up the phone and asked reception to send up a doctor.

I lay back and closed my eyes. I did not want a fuss, I just wanted to be left alone. I did not want to be in England. I did not want to see a doctor, or Maurice, or anybody. But I was relieved that finally someone else was in charge.

'The doctor will be here in half an hour. Meanwhile I will stay and keep you company. I can tell you all that we did with your sister, Leah, when she was in London. She is a wonderful person. We had such a good time together.'

'Where's Maurice?' I whispered.

'Mr. Goodman is contacting him. He should be here this evening. Now you are not to worry about anything. We have all the wedding arrangements in hand. Do you have a wedding dress, Harriett?'

'Of course.'

'May I see it? Has it long sleeves?'

'*Does she want to check up on me?*' I thought, offended that she did not have the grace to trust me to know what was right.

'It is in the closet,' I said from the bed.

'What's a closet?' She sounded cross.

'A cupboard,' I replied.

She opened the wardrobe door and held out my dress.

'Oh, that is beautiful!' she exclaimed. 'Where did you get it?'

'I had it made for me,' I said proudly. 'It cost £9.'

To my astonishment she exclaimed, 'For goodness sake, don't tell anyone! Say it came from Worth.'

'Why?' I could not understand why I should lie about my gorgeous dress.

At that moment the doctor arrived. Mrs. Goodman stood to leave.

'Now you take care of yourself. I want you looking your best for the big day,' she said. 'I will arrange for your bouquet. All you have to do is recover from your journey. Don't you worry about a thing.'

She waved at me from the door and was gone.

The doctor confirmed that I was only bruised and that time would heal the pain. I groaned inwardly, feeling very sorry for myself.

'He is not right,' I thought. 'Time will never heal the pain I am in.'

CHAPTER 25

London (April 1940)

The telephone rang in my hotel room.

'Harriett darling, it's Maurice. I am downstairs. I am coming up.'

'I can't wait,' I said sourly.

When I opened the door, the man I was to marry stood outside beaming at me.

'Darling Goldilocks!' He held me at arms length, then kissed me. 'You are here at last!'

I glared at him.

'I'm turning around and going straight back!' I said.

He put his arm around my shoulder and sat me down on the bed, sitting beside me.

'I know what leaving Palestine means to you, believe me. You have had a traumatic journey to get here. You arrive in a country at war. You are worn out. I don't blame you for feeling angry.'

'I'm not angry,' I retorted. 'I am in pain and I am unhappy.'

'Look, this is for you.' He took a box from his pocket and opened it. Inside was a large single diamond and platinum ring. 'Put it on.'

'No, thank you. It's much too large for me. I shall never wear it.' I turned my head away to hide my tears.

'Well, never mind. Keep it anyway.' He was bemused and shook his head at me.

'If you had asked me I would have chosen a green one.' I thought I should give some explanation for my refusal.

'An emerald? Well, this is more usual for an engagement ring. Let me slip it on for you.'

He took my left hand in his and slid on the ring.

'It fits!' he said delightedly.

I looked at the huge stone on my finger. It was not at all what I would have worn My parents had never felt the need to display wealth openly by wearing jewellery. I was brought up to think that was rather vulgar.

'It sparkles,' I said, trying not to sound ungracious.

'Now you can show it off to everybody.'

'I do not wish to show off!'

Maurice looked very hurt.

'I'm sorry. It is lovely,' I said, not wanting to make things worse. 'And I have a wedding present for you.'

'A prayer shawl made in Jerusalem.' I produced a large tallit, with deep blue stripes and long tassels and fringes.

'Oh, Harriett!' He stood up, unfolded it reverently, threw it around his shoulders and, with his eyes closed, said a short prayer. 'I shall treasure this always. It will go with me to my grave.'

I grimaced.

'Now get dressed. We will have a quiet dinner together and tomorrow I will drive you to see my family.'

'I have already met your mother,' I said.

The house in Brondesbury was filled with Maurice's relatives and friends. As he ushered me in to the gathering, Ettie Goodman, charming, warm and ladylike came forward to embrace me.

'I would like you to be the daughter I never had,' she said kissing my cheek. 'You *must* call me Mama.'

I tried to be as polite as possible.

'I am afraid I can't do that. I already have a mother and that is what I call her.'

She raised her chin. 'Well, call me Mother then.'

Maurice's father, Lazarus, was also there to greet me.

'Can you call me *Daddy?*' he enquired.

I laughed. 'Of course I will. I have *never* called my father that!'

Strangers gathered around to shake my hand. They stared at my left hand where I had surreptitiously twisted the diamond towards my palm.

'May I see your ring?' Each in turn asked the same question.

I found it very distasteful, but Maurice's Uncle Harry and Aunt Miriam, a lovely Swiss lady, must have sensed my feelings because they hastened to my side. She put her hand gently on my arm.

'It is the custom here to show your engagement ring. They are only trying to be kind,' she explained.

'A toast to the bride and groom!' someone shouted, and everybody raised their glasses.

I was handed a glass of champagne which I drank before exclaiming 'I don't usually drink!'

At my side, Maurice slipped his arm around my waist and held me close for a moment. His younger brother, Harold, had arrived from Cambridge University to join the party.

'Well done, brother!' He shook my hand and clapped Maurice on the back.

'He is the best man,' said Maurice, grinning at him.

I suddenly thought. 'May I ask your Uncle Harry and his wife to stand in for my parents under the Chuppa? They seem so kind,'

'I am sure they will feel honoured,' said Maurice.

Everything was organised and fell into place. Invitations were printed for the wedding on 17th April at the Grosvenor House Hotel. The religious ceremony would be held in the small ballroom, followed by a Tea Dance with Sidney Lipton's orchestra. After the wedding we would stay in Brondesbury with the in-laws, then spend time looking for a flat of our own on our return from honeymoon.

That evening Maurice escorted me back to the hotel. Once we were alone in the lift, my fiancé bent to kiss me goodnight. Suddenly, we were holding each other closely and kissing passionately as the lift stopped on my floor.

'Darling, I'm going to leave you now,' said Maurice at the door to my room. 'I'm taking you to meet the Rabbi tomorrow. He wants to make certain you know what you are letting yourself in for.'

I stood on my toes and kissed him again. 'I do,' I said.

'Now be a good girl and get a good night's sleep,' said the man who was to marry me.

The following morning, a hand-written letter awaited me in reception:

Darlingest,

You will think you are way back in Tel Aviv when you receive this and you'll probably swear (don't forget you are a lady!) when you realise that this letter-writing seems to be interminable. I don't know whether or not it is an instinctive faith in the greater value of the written word: I don't know if it is a persistent shyness (which, too, we share) at the thought of putting things into coarse words. Explain it how you like but be tolerant, please, because I just want to write one or two things, sleepy though I am, and I do want you to get them into that lovely, active but slightly stupid brain of yours.

I have told you before that I appreciate fully what it has meant to you to leave your parents, your sister, and brother and Mattie, to leave Palestine (which I know you love) and travel by such tortuous means in war-time to England to marry me. I fail utterly and truthfully to discover any single feature about me which might deserve such sacrifices on your part. I know that I am not (to use a vulgar expression) worthy of you, unless, of course, it be that I love you dearly and have loved you for as long as I can remember. Nothing mattered before I met you. I love you, darling, just simply as you are.

Bless you, sweetheart. All my love,
'Well, whom do you think?'

The night before my wedding I slept in the Goodman's home. I awoke early and went downstairs for a cigarette. As I inhaled deeply, Lazarus Goodman appeared and gently took the cigarette out of my hand.

'You're supposed to be fasting,' he said.

I blushed and ran upstairs.

Downstairs I could hear the household beginning to bustle, but I stayed hidden in my bedroom until Ettie Goodman entered.

'Harriett, this is for you,' said Ettie, handing me a small box. 'Something blue.' Inside was a frilly garter with blue ribbon.

'What fun!' I said, as I slipped it high on my thigh.

At eleven, Ettie Goodman and I were driven, with all my paraphernalia, to Grosvenor House Hotel where a room had been booked for us. Everything went like clockwork. The hairdresser arrived together with a beautician who both went to work on me. Mrs. Goodman's dressmaker arrived to assist in dressing the bride. One or two other ladies of the family, including Aunt Miriam, joined to support me before my wedding. The room was bustling with excitement.

'No one need fast,' decided Ettie Goodman, ordering a huge platter of sandwiches. 'Not even you, Harriett!'

She was a lady of great generosity, and we all tucked in gratefully.

When the bouquet was delivered it was not at all what I would have chosen. Stiff wax-like arum lilies lay wrapped in tissue paper. They felt all wrong for me. I had expected a trail of orange blossom and was disappointed. But then this was England and not Palestine. Everything was much more formal over here.

I stood fully dressed before the long mirror, seeing a beautiful bride in the reflection. I had come a long way from being the gangling teenager, shy and reticent. My upbringing and my parents' deep love for Judaism and each other, had given me the solid base from which I vowed to create a good Jewish home.

The Chupa, the wedding canopy, was set up in the small ballroom. At one o'clock, I stood beside Maurice before Dayan Lazarus and Rabbi Harris Cohen, the family Rabbi. Blessings were sung for the bride and groom, after which there was a short address by Rabbi Cohen. Then the goblet of wine was blessed, from which we both sipped.

According to custom, Maurice placed the wedding ring on the first finger of my right hand saying: Haray Aht ('Harriett,' he whispered) Mekudeshet Li Betabat Zu Kedat Moshe Ve Yisrael. Then he repeated in English: 'You are consecrated unto me by this ring according to the law of Moses and of Israel.'

It was for me to say nothing.

After the marriage contract was read aloud in Hebrew, and English, Dayan Lazarus sang the seven blessings.

Finally, a small velvet bag containing a glass was placed on the floor. Maurice stamped to break it, as is the custom at Jewish weddings. Everyone shouted aloud 'Mazeltov!' - Good Luck! Then Maurice lifted my veil and kissed me.

Everything was exactly as my parents would have wanted it.

The seventy guests applauded us warmly as we turned around to join them for a tea-dance.

'Only two people here know me,' I said to Maurice wistfully. 'You and Jack Sloane.'

'Everybody will soon get to know you and love you,' Maurice assured me as we sat down together with my in-laws.

Sidney Lipton came across to ask what tune we would like for the first dance. A new song had just come out which expressed my feelings exactly. Overcome with yearning for my dearest parents I immediately suggested *My Heart Belongs to Daddy!* He looked quizzical.

'I think *It's a Hap, Hap, Happy Day!* would be more suitable,' he advised.

He turned to conduct the orchestra for the first dance. As Maurice and I took to the floor we were quickly joined by smiling wedding guests.

'*When are we going to dance at your wedding?* How many times had I been asked that question?'

'*Now!*' I grinned to myself.

Despite the absence of my family, it was a happy day. After the reception, Maurice drove me to the Savoy Hotel where we were to spend our wedding night.

That evening as I stood by our window overlooking the Thames it was strange to think that I was in London, in a country at war, hundreds of miles from my family. And I was a married woman.

*

So long ago.

As I sit reliving the past and reading through correspondence that I have kept all these years, one last letter reminds me how it was:

29ᵗʰ May 1940

My darling Harriett,

I haven't written to you for such a long time....the dividing line which took place on April 17ᵗʰ was so miraculously wonderful that I cannot honestly say that I have come out of the dream to realise this is all true and that my hopes and prayers are really granted. You are and always will be the dearest creature, the loveliest most beautiful girl imaginable...your beautiful face, your rosy velvety cheeks and your burning blue-green eyes, your sweet lips and your so very attractive smile, all alight and glowing with what I pray is true happiness. ...If only you had believed me long ago you would not have delayed to come and marry me: because I told you we would be happy together. May we always be happy for very many years to come.

Bless you, my sweetheart.

Your Maurice.

He always did write the most romantic and persuasive letters. That was one of the reasons why I had married him.

Postscript (1940-1946)

On 10th May 1940, Germany invaded Belgium and Holland. It was fate that I had arrived safely in England in the nick of time. On 14th May 1940, the German Luftwaffe bombed Rotterdam to force the capitulation of Holland. After five days the Dutch surrendered. My thoughts were with the kindly Dutchmen who had accompanied me to Paris, and with all the Jews who were now under Nazi control.

I was young, energetic and eager to do my bit. I knew that I was in the right place at the right time. We were going to win this war.

*

In May 1945, at the end of the war in Europe, all Americans abroad were offered repatriation to the States. Esther and her family, together with my parents, returned to New Haven to be reunited with the family. J.L. and my mother stayed in America for a year until my father decided it was time to return to the Holy Land.

In the summer of 1946, on their way back to Herzlia, my parents arrived to stay with me in London for a short while. Here they were introduced to their new grandson, Leslie.

My mother, looking delighted, sat with my baby on her lap. She smiled serenely at my father.

'Now you are a mature woman, Harriett,' said my father. 'Do you begin to understand what happiness is?'

'That I should be healthy, and have healthy babies?' I said. 'You are right, Papa. I am beginning to appreciate your philosophy. You have a great understanding of life.'

'Well, we live in a new world, one far different from the times when I was born,' said J.L. 'There are still obstacles to overcome. But we look forward to being in the Holy Land when the Jewish State is established. It *will* come about.'

He was emphatic as he continued.

'That is my dream, as you know, Harriett. And to see you settled and safe. That is my dream for all of my children.'

Epilogue

H arriett arrived in England just a few weeks before France fell to Germany. She and Maurice lived in London throughout the Blitz and wartime restrictions. They had two children, Leslie and Talya, both born after the war. Harriett and Maurice were married for thirty four years.

In 1942, when America entered the war, Sol joined the US Army in Palestine and served as a sergeant in the Middle East. At the end of the war he was repatriated to the States to be discharged. He never returned to live in Palestine.

Rhea, Leah and Rose all married and left children who still live in the States. Esther and Mattie returned to the USA with their son after the war. Esther and all her children live in the States.

Sarah Freda Gold died in 1954 when she was seventy. She was buried in Herzlia.

J.L., who was ten years older than his wife, remained in Herzlia until he was eighty-one when the family decided he could no longer live alone. He agreed to return to the States to live with Esther on condition that when he died he would be buried alongside his beloved wife. He died in January 1964.

In January 1964, Harriett waited alone in a transit lounge at Heathrow Airport for her brother, Sol, to fly over from the

States. He was accompanying their father's coffin to Israel, where J.L. had been Mayor of Azor Gimmel for many years. When Sol arrived he was able to spend an hour at the airport with Harriett, both very sad and near to tears. After they parted, Sol took his father's body back to Herzlia. There all the old settlers and many other people came to pay their respects at the funeral when J.L. was buried beside his beloved wife, Sarah. Harriett returned to sit in mourning alone in London.

None of J.L's issue remain in Eretz Israel today, but he had lived to see the establishment of the State of Israel in 1948. It was his dream come true. A number of his children and grandchildren have retained a close relationship with Israel and some have homes there.

In 1968, when Harriett and Leah were on a visit together to Israel, they were approached on the steps of the Dan Hotel by an American tourist.

'I can hear you are English,' said the lady. 'Do you by any chance know someone living in England called Harriett Gold? I have been trying to get in contact with her, but so far I have had no success.'

'I was Harriett Gold before I became Mrs. Goodman,' said Harriett, astonished at the coincidence.

The lady embraced her delightedly.

'I'm Mildred's sister,' she said. 'She kept all those letters you sent her so many years ago. I have been longing to find you so that I can return them to the writer. I am sure you could write your memoirs with them.'